5 Ways to Get the Most from *Profit in Plain Sight*

Never have to say "we don't have the budget for that!" again!

1. **Thrive...** by building a strong bottom line as you implement the Action Plans within as a team

2. **Build Loyalty...** by gifting customers with a copy to help them succeed

3. **Close Business Faster...** by using this book as a sales premium

4. **Open Doors Sooner...** by sending prospects a copy as a conversation starter

5. **Sleep Soundly...** when you gift a copy to your suppliers & industry associations to help them serve you better

Claim your special perks for multiple copies at www.ProfitInPlainSight.com

It's *your* time... to sell more products & services... to more customers... at higher prices... & lower costs... as you innovate to lead your market... in less time than you're spending on email.

- With My Compliments -

Help others enjoy this book by posting a review on Amazon.

For Rita
Let's collaborate on
"F & C" & go
make good things happen!

Anne C Graw

Anne Graham delivers a book with insightful practical advice that will help leaders immediately be more effective. It combines a well-thought-out framework and tools with real-world business acumen that will help any professional find the solutions in plain sight for their business

> ~ Heather MacKenzie, Director of Marketing,
> Belden International Inc.

Only read this book if you are truly interested in having a sustainably profitable company full of highly engaged people. Don't bother if you're satisfied with being mediocre

> ~ Jim Sellner, VP Learnings and Applications,
> VIVOTeam Consulting Inc.

When you don't know How but you Should, reach for *Profit In Plain Sight*. Simple concepts, clearly explained – you will wonder why you never thought of it that way before.

> ~ Pat Bjerrisgaard, Senior Director, Global
> Employee Engagement, SAP

Practical, insightful and action-oriented. Every page is filled with thought-provoking ideas or insights.

> ~ Leslie Meingast, CEO, The Personnel Department

Ouch!!! *Profit In Plain Sight* made me take a hard and honest look into my company and helped me recognise what is not working, the book helped me to be honest with myself, my company, shareholders, employees and really "work" with my clients to build a superior client-supplier relationship, based in value conversations. The book provides great advice on how to make the changes happen, and these did happen. I am so glad to have this book as a guide to keep growing with passion and be profitable in doing so.

> ~ Laura Aveledo, Product Marketing Manager,
> Moneris Solutions

Anne has put together practical, proven ways to grow your business ... every business owner and manager will find great ideas that will jump-start their business quickly.

~ George Noroian, Founder, Giant Leap
Management Solutions

Anne Graham challenges business leaders to attack the myths which prevent businesses from reaching their full profit potential, and provides thoughtful guidance on how to deliver outstanding results. *Profit in Plain Sight* is not the flavor of the month. It's practical, relevant and timeless.

~ Jim Bogusz, Chief Operating Officer, The Beedie Group

There are a lot of gems hidden in plain sight in this book. Anne shows you specific steps and tools she has found to be successful in transforming business performance in a big way. It all starts with passion, profit, and growth. You and your team need to do the work but if you have time to watch TV or do e-mail, you can do this. Buy the book. Read it. And follow the instructions.

~ Doug Wagner, President of Sunwapta Solution

Finally a practical approach to a complex problem. Anne's vision on business is unique and effective.

~ Juan Jose Gonzales, Co-Founder & COO at
Gazelles Growth Institute

Anne is really a thought leader in business. This is a must read for anyone running a business and wants to increase profits by using her clear methods. Awesome!

~ Anthony J. Davis, Owner, Nicoll Davis & Spinella LLP

Profit in Plain Sight ... has amazing potential to help companies and leaders get more to the bottom line with less work.

~ John Cummings, Founder, BodySite Wellness Platform

A valuable "how-to" filled with such great stories that I know Anne has been there and done that. It left me with confidence that it will work for me, too.

~ Hugh R. Alley, P.Eng., President First Line Training Inc.

What a great read. If you are a leader looking for a book that packs a punch of value, guides you through a step-by-step process consistently supported by gobs of research to inspire and motive you to action *Profit In Plain Sight* is for you. I love how Anne peppers insights and actions with tough love leadership questions. Thank you Anne, my profits are soaring because of you!

~ Renée Safrata, CIC, VIVOTeam Consulting Inc.

Through innovative yet uncomplicated thinking, *Profit in Plain Sight* covers the whole gamut involved in transforming any business into a powerhouse. ... *Every* leadership professional at *any* level of *all* organizations will greatly benefit from this information and inspiration packed book.

~ Independent Publisher

PROFIT
IN
PLAIN SIGHT

*The Five Principled Paths
to Passion, Profit,
and Growth*

ANNE GRAHAM

It is not the purpose of this book to repeat all the information that is otherwise available to business leaders, but instead to complement, amplify and supplement other resources. You are urged to seek additional available material and tailor the information to your individual needs.

Every effort has been made to make this book as complete and accurate as possible. However, there may be mistakes, both typographical and in content. Therefore, this text should be used only as a general guide and not as the ultimate source of business information. The author and LVI Publishing shall have neither liability nor responsibility to any person or entity with respect to any loss or damage caused or alleged to have been caused, directly or indirectly, by the information contained in this book.

Library and Archives Canada Cataloguing in Publication

Graham, Anne, 1961–, author

Profit in plain sight : the five principled paths to passion, profit, and growth / Anne Graham.

Includes index.
ISBN 978-0-9867120-4-3 (bound)

1. Profit. 2. Industrial management. I. Title.

HB601.G73 2013   338.5'16   C2013-901775-5

Editing: Catherine Leek of Green Onion Publishing
Interior Design and Formatting: Kim Monteforte of WeMakeBooks.ca
Cover Design: Kim Monteforte of WeMakeBooks.ca

Published by: LVI Publishing
                4132 – 349 West Georgia St.
                Vancouver, BC V6B 3Z6
                www.LVIPublishing.com
                info@LVIPublishing.com
                Phone: (604) 259-9858
                Toll Free: (855) 259-9858

Who's In Charge of Your Future?

There's a problem in our economy today but it's not what we think.

- How often do you find yourself struggling to attract and keep the best customers, or find yourself surprised when business you were counting on suddenly goes to the competition?

- How often do you generate significant top-line revenue growth, and are dismayed that you can't keep it long enough to see it on the bottom line?

- How common is conventional cost cutting in your organization, yet you find that it doesn't have enough impact on your bottom line to really make a difference?

- How often have you invested time and effort in building high quality products and services, only to find that your customer service staff are *still* busy on the phones and handling e-mail complaints from customers all day long?

- How often do you wonder where the next big idea is for your business — and often find your competitors beat you to it?

We hear in the press that companies are sitting on record profits, and while that might be true for some very large companies, it does not reflect the reality for most businesses, whose "Business Bucket Lists" are hurting for lack of profit. Is that you?

But the press also says that before businesses can fully recover and thrive we need different tax structures, different foreign investment rules, more government incentive programs to drive productivity, more protection from foreign competition, and so on. I call that a bad case of the "someone-shoulds" — "someone should" fix everything, so that businesses and our economy can prosper again. Here's the reality of what we hear about "sitting on record profits" and the "someone should" approaches.

- Almost 20% of Fortune 500 companies are *unprofitable* … and unable to contribute to economic growth.[1]

- Only *4 in 10* manufacturers have restored their production or profitability levels beyond the pre-recession levels of 2007.[2]

- Among thousands of senior leaders of small- and medium-sized companies polled, 83% rate their satisfaction with their ability to invest in their businesses as *less than 6 out of 10*, because they don't have the cash flow and profit they need to fund the growth they want.

Yet a select group of companies have overcome the challenges above, and, in fact, their *average* profitability level has increased by almost 37% in the past year alone.[3] Has yours? If not, then common sense solutions in plain sight hold the key to taking charge of your future — solutions that you can implement independently of waiting for someone else to fix the economy.

Let me ask you a question.

On a scale of 1 to 10, how completely ecstatic are you with your current level of profitability? Now, consider what would be possible if you shifted that to an 8 … or a 9 … *or a 10*. Whether you simply want to get back in the black to secure your future, whether you want more profit to invest back into good people, equipment, technology, acquisitions, or whether you want to increase the valuation of your business in preparation for a lucrative merger or sale, *Profit in Plain Sight* can help.

---

[1] *Anne Graham, "Return on People: The Powerful-Yet-Overlooked Benchmark for Transformation" for 2013. Review this report at www.ProfitInPlainSight.com/Benchmark.*

[2] *"An Optimistic Focus on an Uncertain Future" in Industry Week, November 2012 at p. 14.*

We all want to achieve a level of success and certainty. We all want the confidence to move past what the economy says we can or can't have. We all want to be rewarded for all the hard work and effort we put in.

So it's time for leaders at *all levels* of *every* organization to take charge of the future and trigger the cycle of prosperity — to build great companies that can weather today's economic turmoil and thrive in the uncertainties of tomorrow. You can be part of a ground-swell of profit and growth that leads the way and changes our world. Or you can continue to struggle with stubborn market challenges preventing achievement of that full potential. If you're a high-integrity leader ready to step up and build a better future, you're in the right place.

Get ready to move the needle in your business.

I'm going to show you exactly how you can get out from behind your desk, put some play back in your day, and some serious bucks on your bottom line. That's the way you can do your part to be engaged in building both your business and your war chest so that your organization will not just survive, but thrive despite whatever increasing rates of change, economic turmoil, and globalization can throw at it. And it's how you'll surround yourself with great people who share your vision and want to help you make it happen. You're going to transform your business, and your life, in less time than you're spending on e-mail today.

You can do it. You will succeed.

Anne Graham
Vancouver, Canada
January 2, 2014

Table of Contents

PART II Shift to Practicalities

Prepare to Transform Your Most Persistent Market Challenges into Passion, Profit, and Growth

... With Five Principled Paths that Deliver Results in Less Time than You're Currently Spending on E-mail

> **How much easier** would igniting passion, profit, and growth be if everyone in your business embraced change and became part of it?
>
> **What would be possible** if transforming your business felt more like play than like work?
>
> **How quickly could you turn good intentions into tangible results** if you simply could take small steps that require less time than you are devoting to e-mail in a given day?

IBM is a legendary company, not only because of its enduring success for over 100 years in the fast-changing world of technology, but because it leads its category *by a factor of four* in terms of profitability and continues to transform itself to generate growth opportunities. Customers are incredibly loyal, the company has a stellar reputation for quality, and, as the holder of more patents than any other high-technology company, its strengths in innovation are readily apparent. It seems that IBM has found ways to conquer some stubborn challenges, doesn't it?

But it didn't start that way. IBM's roots go back to the 1880s and at one time its products consisted of employee time-keeping systems, weigh scales, automatic meat slicers, coffee grinders, and punched card equipment. Hardly the glamorous "Creating a Smarter Planet" organization we know today.

IBM's secrets to success came from an unlikely resource who was named President in 1915: Thomas J. Watson, the second in command at National Cash Register. With just a few practical tenets, Watson laid down the enduring foundation for IBM's success — a focus on the customer and on customer service, a sales culture that built trust and respect, and an environment that instilled pride and loyalty into every worker. The result? Passion, profit, and growth, with integrity. In the 1990s, IBM had to reinvent itself or risk becoming irrelevant in the marketplace, which it did by reemphasizing its customer focus and creating clarity in its positioning. In the 2000s, it had to reinvent itself again as the competitive landscape shifted once more, which it did by emphasizing its role in providing integrated solutions, not merely products.

This is not a book about IBM. But as subsequent legendary leaders have proven, those enduring, practical tenets can serve every business well.

How Many of these Stubborn Market Challenges Are Grinding You Down?

Each year a variety of organizations publish lists of the Top 10 CEO Challenges based on polling business owners and leaders. And inevitably, five stubborn market-related issues keep coming up again and again on these lists, although the order may shift from year to year:

1. Earning Customer Loyalty and Retention
2. Generating Sustained and Steady Top-Line Growth
3. Ensuring Bottom-Line Growth in Profit
4. Building a Corporate Reputation for Quality Products and Services

5. Stimulating Innovation and Creativity and Enabling Entrepreneurship

Why don't we ever get traction and put those Challenges behind us? Because 70 years of thought leadership in the business press, from universities and in executive programs, has left us with more *shoulds* than *hows* and a lot of flavor-of-the-month distractions that sound promising but are hard to translate into bottom-line impact.

Let's change that.

This Book Is for You When ...

... most of the books you've read are sitting on your shelf and have not had any impact on your business;

... some of the books you've read have inspired you but you struggled when you tried to put them into practice because the author shared the *shoulds* but left you to figure out the *hows*; and

... you've tried to implement ideas in the past as an army of one only to run out of steam, run out of time, or run out of focus when you find yourself spending more time trying to get people to change and get on board than actually implementing anything.

Move Beyond the Myths

Here's your wake-up call and a bold promise.

MYTH #1
We're Too Busy

FACT: All of us are busy. None of us have spare time. Or do we? Over 90% of executives polled admit that they spend between 1 and 2 hours a day on e-mail ... often more. So here's your wake-up call: unless you work in the order entry department, e-mail does *not* move the needle in your business because it does *not* create cash flow, profit, or growth. In fact, it leaves you working everyone else's agenda when, as a leader, it is up to you to set the direction and lead by doing. E-mail is a nice, easy, reactive way to start the day and waste most of the morning. And it's killing your company.

MYTH #2
We Have to Be "Always On"

FACT: We're tethered to responding instantaneously to our phones, our e-mail, and other interruptions, and there are times when that's appropriate, but more often it's simply busy work. I'm not saying that you have to abandon e-mail — it's a part of our lives in the 21st century, just as the telephone and voice mail became a reality in the 20th. But what is currently in your in-box or on your priority list that is *more important* than securing the future of your business for your employees, your family, and your community? What's more important than building a profitable, growing business that can weather any economic turmoil that global change can throw at it?

MYTH #3
There's No Way Out

FACT: The noise is getting louder now that texting and social media elements are also in the mix of e-mail, voice mail, and more. Yet one simple shift is all that's required to completely transform noise into results, and I invite you to share Appendix 1 with your entire organization to help them make that shift.

In the meantime, here's my bold promise.

> **If you have time for e-mail, you have time to once and for all overcome the stubborn business challenges holding you back.**

When you follow the Solutions in Plain Sight outlined in this book and access the Rapid Results Resources that ensure you never have to waste precious time reinventing the wheel, you will transform your business in less time than you're currently spending on e-mail.

First, Expand Your Thinking to Close the Gap

Our biggest challenge as business leaders at all levels is simply to overcome the thinking that's kept us stuck with those Challenges. Many of us were taught old-world thinking, long before today's realities of the Internet, globalization, recurring corporate scandals, all-too-frequent recessions, and a rate of change that's difficult to keep up with. It's time to hold our beliefs, myths, and common practices up to a very harsh light of uncommon sense and retool for the future. It's time to replace them with a road map that delivers results. This first section, Possibilities, is going to give you three powerful tools to do just that.

Most businesses won't succeed in making the shift. They'll remain mired in the "we've always done it this way" paradigm, because they simply won't invest the time and energy to be open to new approaches, and they won't take the time to build a road map that takes them to their Possibilities, step by step. They'll continue to default back to "business as usual," because they think it's easier, even though they know it's not working, and they need a new approach. Unfortunately, they're unknowingly making their lives and the lives of everyone in the organization more difficult, and more uncertain.

Take a look at the shapes Figure 1. How many forms of transportation can you spot? Look carefully, as the shapes hold the key to your transformation. How many did you see? What were they? (Go to Appendix 2 for the answer.)

Figure 1: HOW MANY FORMS OF TRANSPORTATION
DO YOU SEE IN THESE SHAPES?

Rapid Results Resources: Put some energy into your regular meetings and start the process of Transformation with "The 101 Questions You MUST Ask Your Leadership Team." Use a couple of the questions every week to get your team thinking about Passion, Profit, and Growth, and to get their creative juices flowing. Download your copy at www.ProfitInPlainSight.com/101Questions.

 ## Solutions in Plain Sight: Inform. Inspire. Motivate. Systematically Transform.

By opening the cover of *Profit in Plain Sight*, you've already taken your first step to becoming more open, more focused, and more successful. You've taken your first step towards creating a process for sustainable levels of increased profits. And you've taken your first step that will differentiate your business from your competitors' when you implement well. Just keep turning the pages to make it happen.

 ### SOLUTION IN PLAIN SIGHT #1
Infuse Your Employees With Possibilities

What does it mean to *Infuse* employees? It means embedding the desire to be part of something more, to be the best, to behave every day in ways that add value to your customers, and to earn profit with integrity that will help the entire company grow and succeed in the future.

Figure 2: INFUSE YOUR EMPLOYEES WHEN YOU INFORM, INSPIRE, MOTIVATE AND TRANSFORM

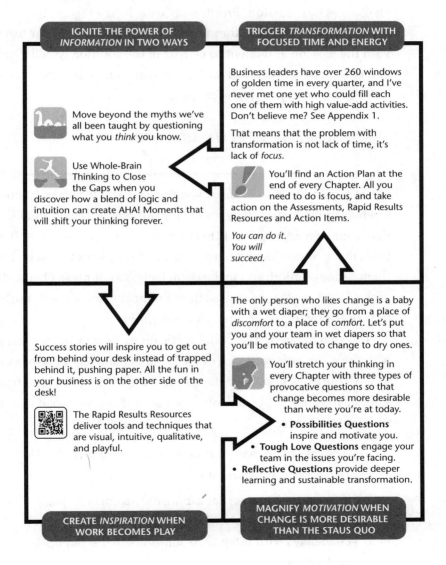

IGNITE THE POWER OF *INFORMATION* IN TWO WAYS

Move beyond the myths we've all been taught by questioning what you *think* you know.

Use Whole-Brain Thinking to Close the Gaps when you discover how a blend of logic and intuition can create AHA! Moments that will shift your thinking forever.

TRIGGER *TRANSFORMATION* WITH FOCUSED TIME AND ENERGY

Business leaders have over 260 windows of golden time in every quarter, and I've never met one yet who could fill each one of them with high value-add activities. Don't believe me? See Appendix 1.

That means that the problem with transformation is not lack of time, it's lack of *focus*.

You'll find an Action Plan at the end of every Chapter. All you need to do is focus, and take action on the Assessments, Rapid Results Resources and Action Items.

You can do it.
You will
succeed.

Success stories will inspire you to get out from behind your desk instead of trapped behind it, pushing paper. All the fun in your business is on the other side of the desk!

The Rapid Results Resources deliver tools and techniques that are visual, intuitive, qualitative, and playful.

The only person who likes change is a baby with a wet diaper; they go from a place of *discomfort* to a place of *comfort*. Let's put you and your team in wet diapers so that you'll be motivated to change to dry ones.

You'll stretch your thinking in every Chapter with three types of provocative questions so that change becomes more desirable than where you're at today.

- **Possibilities Questions** inspire and motivate you.
- **Tough Love Questions** engage your team in the issues you're facing.
- **Reflective Questions** provide deeper learning and sustainable transformation.

CREATE *INSPIRATION* WHEN WORK BECOMES PLAY

MAGNIFY *MOTIVATION* WHEN CHANGE IS MORE DESIRABLE THAN THE STAUS QUO

It means engaging them with the Drivers of Transformation that you'll see in Part I, Possibilities, which will give them the powerful AHA! Moments of information, inspiration, and motivation.

It means involving them in creating the road map forward, because information, inspiration, motivation, and good intentions need to be turned into action before you can transform stubborn challenges into Passion, Profit, and Growth (see Figure 2).

People support what they create. When you *Infuse* your teams with the passion and talent to be part of the solution, you'll divide and conquer the workload and transform your profit and growth more easily than you might imagine.

 SOLUTION IN PLAIN SIGHT #2
Enthuse Your Customers

What does it mean to *Enthuse* your customers? It means creating an environment where they love doing business with you and know that your success is part of their success, because you save them time, make or save them money, solve real problems for them, give them peace of mind, and make them feel good. It means being the path of least resistance and getting it right the first time. It means they're happy to pay for the value you provide.

It's what happens in Part II, Practicalities, when you take action with the systematic approach of the Profit in Plain Sight Framework to solve the five stubborn challenges that are holding you back from leading your market by industriously activating your road map to success (see Figure 3).

1. Activate the power of *Infused* employees with the Three Drivers of Transformation.

2. Trigger the factors that *Enthuse* customers as you systematically overcome five stubborn market-driven challenges with integrated solutions that build upon each other.

3. Achieve Passion, Profit, and Growth ... in less time than you're spending on e-mail.

Figure 3: **THE PROFIT IN PLAIN SIGHT FRAMEWORK**

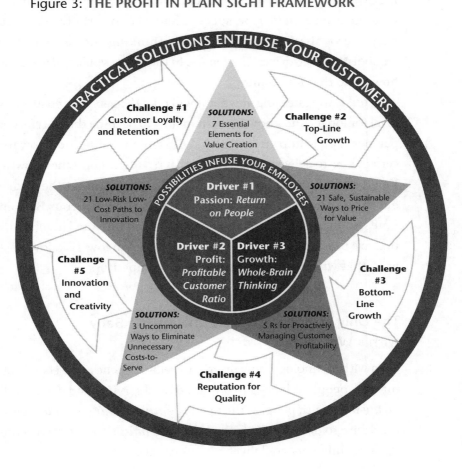

SOLUTION IN PLAIN SIGHT #3
Overcome Your Biggest Obstacles

Right now you may be thinking you don't have the time. Your people aren't onside. You have other priorities that need your attention and focus. You're uncertain of whether you can make a commitment to see this through. You don't believe that significant profit increases are possible in your business or in your industry. Hogwash!

Bringing the voices of your customers into your organization is a powerful, counterintuitive, yet proven, approach to see what's possible from a *tactical* perspective and will powerfully move you past "we've always done it this way" thinking with each of five stubborn market-driven challenges. In this book, you'll learn exactly how to do that for results.

You'll stop guessing at what it will take to keep your customers loyal for longer and know for certain how to become their preferred partner. You'll stop guessing what they might value and know for certain how to deliver value to them that results in Top-Line Growth. You'll stop applying bandaids to quality issues and get the sludge out of your system to stop the profit leaks and grow your Bottom Line. And you'll know exactly how to avoid "me too" inventions that are passing for innovation and innovate in low-risk, low-cost ways that will set you apart from your competitors.

The Only Person Who Likes Change Is a Baby with a Wet Diaper

Even with technology, globalization, credit crunches, and economic turmoil, people still need to buy goods and services and people still do business with people. The need to *enthuse your customers* with the desire to do business with you and to *infuse your staff* with the passion and talent to deliver never changes.

What does need to change is how you tackle those five stubborn market-driven challenges, and therein lies the stumbling block.

Your people can't buy into the typical approach of an endless stream of unrelated tasks, so-called best practices (which *don't* differentiate you from your competitors), flavor-of-the-month management and proverbial silver bullets. Over 90% of business owners, leaders, and key employees polled admit they get lost chasing bright shiny objects, and those are simply the equivalent of trying to change nice, dry, comfortable diapers to icky wet diapers that don't make sense to your people. Uncertainty, seemingly wasted time, wasted effort, confusion, and the feeling of a lack of progress simply causes fear and resistance.

Harvard Professor W. Earl Sasser was the first to refer to the plethora of stand-alone tactics as "Kidney Stone Management" (his lengthy list back in the 1990s has only expanded with time). We've trained our staff to expect that whatever new idea is out there, it's a kidney stone — *it will only cause them pain for a while, it will pass, and business as usual can return.* No wonder our people are burned-out and skeptical when so many new initiatives are launched, so many seem important, and so many run out of steam. Explain Kidney Stone Management to your executive and management teams at all levels. You're guaranteed a few rueful chuckles of recognition and an AHA! Moment that indicates that approach is no longer going to be part of your leadership practices.

That's the reason *Profit in Plain Sight* will make a difference when others haven't — solving these Challenges for good comes down to realizing that you're in wet diapers and wanting the dry ones you'll get by shifting the way you do business. Dry diapers are the result of implementing the step-by-step road map of over 57 detailed, value-add Profit and Growth Accelerators for *near term yet sustainable* Passion, Profit, and Growth.

When your people have a mental map of where they're going, how they're going to get there (see Figure 3), Kidney Stone Management is no longer a problem and they will be informed, inspired, and motivated to get into the dry diapers. A *systematic and integrated process* rather than a series of disconnected events will consistently create successes and a sense of forward momentum and progress — the transformation you're looking for.

You Don't Have to Go It Alone

Unsuccessful businesspeople try to go it alone, reluctant to show their weakness by asking for help. Successful businesspeople ask for help all the time. They call it getting input and they know the value of *not* reinventing the wheel. *Profit in Plain Sight* is the *window* to Rapid Results Resources that are not just *shoulds* but specific *hows* — proven step-by-step instructions plus additional proven strategies and tactics that are beyond the scope of this book. They deliver results more rapidly and easily than you might imagine.

They deliver *smart* practices specifically implemented in the context of your unique company. All you have to do is commit to transforming conventional *passive reading* into *active learning* for results.

Every business leader who has succeeded in doubling their profitability or more — in less than one year, in less time than they and their team were spending on e-mail — has identified obstacles to success. And as they began the process, they found that each and every obstacle dissolved with the straightforward, practical approaches laid out in this book. At this point, all you need to do is finish reading the next two pages, and take the actions outlined. Then, turn the page and do it again. That's it. Are you with me?

Summary

We've all heard that you can lead a horse to water but you can't make it drink. But I always say that you *can* make the horse thirsty or make the water sweeter. From the sheer fact that you're reading *Profit in Plain Sight,* I know you're thirsty.

Make Your Horses Thirsty Too

Embracing a process to transform challenges into opportunities doesn't come from rigorous change management processes that try to force-fit people into a change that they haven't bought into. That's just leading the horse to water. Instead, it comes from naturally leading your team where you want them to go by building an *infused* culture that thirsts for excellence and that reflects their desire to find the easiest and most effective ways to achieve that end. When you share this book throughout your organization, you'll help lead your teams' thirst for where you want them to go.

Make the Water Sweeter

Sweeter water means helping you and your organization find ways to streamline complexity and stay focused on what really drives your business forward. That's where the systematic Profit in Plain Sight Framework is extremely valuable — bite-sized modules are easy to implement, in less time than you're currently spending on e-mail. Make the process painless and make the water sweet when you take an integrated approach rather than succumbing to Kidney Stone Management.

I've spent time in the trenches "doing," and even longer with the responsibilities of leading others. I've experienced the frustration of dealing with these Challenges over and over, just as you have. I've used every one of these Solutions in Plain Sight, as a leader in large and small companies and with my consulting clients. They've worked across a broad range of industries and they'll work for you too.

Simply. Accelerate Your Results

There is really only *one* theme to this book — driving Passion, Profit, and Growth. We're going to put many lenses on that theme, but never lose sight of that as our goal.

There are only *two* outcomes you need to achieve in order to realize Passion, Profit, and Growth — *enthusing* your customers, and *infusing* your employees. I'll show you what you need to do to accomplish both.

There are Three Drivers of Transformation that serve as wet diapers to motivate change and, in Part I, you'll see Possibilities as you learn how to activate them to kick-start the process and help you measure success and progress.

There are 15 practical, actionable Solutions in Plain Sight in this book and a total of 57 Profit and Growth Accelerators in the Profit in Plain Sight Framework. In Part II, Shift to Practicalities, you'll see your Profit in Plain Sight road map unfold as we tackle each of the five stubborn market-driven challenges.

Whether you take action on every Challenge or cherry-pick just those that are holding your business back the most, you will see impact on your Profit. You'll impact the Passion your teams bring to the business. And you'll sow the seeds for Growth.

There are no quick fixes … but Rapid Results are within your reach.

You *can* reach and exceed your goals. You *can* secure your business from the ups and downs of economic turmoil, and invest in everything you need to take your business to the next level and help drive our economy forward. You *can* finally feel confident in your plan for the future.

If Not You, Who? If Not Now, When?

Work is slogging it out in isolation; *play* is getting support to achieve breakthroughs and feeling a sense of progress. So go ahead and put some play back in your day and some bucks on your bottom line.

This Works. You Can Do It. You Will Succeed.

Take these Actions

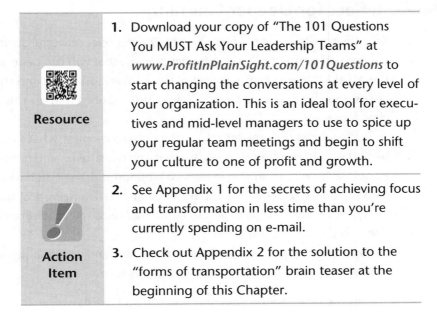

Resource

1. Download your copy of "The 101 Questions You MUST Ask Your Leadership Teams" at *www.ProfitInPlainSight.com/101Questions* to start changing the conversations at every level of your organization. This is an ideal tool for executives and mid-level managers to use to spice up your regular team meetings and begin to shift your culture to one of profit and growth.

Action Item

2. See Appendix 1 for the secrets of achieving focus and transformation in less time than you're currently spending on e-mail.

3. Check out Appendix 2 for the solution to the "forms of transportation" brain teaser at the beginning of this Chapter.

Small Steps. Big Impact!

Five Minutes, Five Questions:
Reflect for Deeper Learning

Reflective questions at the end of every Chapter offer powerful deeper learning on how your thinking is changing, so that you can generate the AHA! Moments to break free of the conventional thinking that keeps you stuck when trying to solve five stubborn market-driven challenges.

Reflection simply means taking the time to monitor what's happening in your own mind, evaluate what you're learning, and ponder what is shifting or changing in terms of your attitudes and behaviors, with the goal of eventually building a new mental framework of how things work. This will allow you to continually add relevant information and discard the irrelevant.

Your first step is *internal* transformation, to identify what attitudes have already shifted and what behaviors will follow.

But the reflective process only works if you use it.

Ask yourself these questions right now:

1. How can I use the reframing approach I saw in the brain teaser as a metaphor for opportunities hidden in our business?

   _____

   _____

2. Which items on the list of five stubborn market-driven challenges are top of mind for me right now — and why?

   _____

   _____

3. How effectively are we solving those challenges today?

   _____

   _____

4. How often do our people see our efforts as Kidney Stones because we fail to give them the big picture with a road map for implementation?

_____

_____

5. How committed am I to create an environment where my horses are thirsty and the water is sweet?

_____

_____

Inform. Inspire. Motivate. Transform.
Enthuse. Infuse.

Are you ready to get started with the Three Drivers of Transformation that deliver big wake-up calls and pave the way to transform your business more quickly and easily than you might imagine?

If you prefer, you can go right to whichever Challenge is your greatest burning issue today, and then work backwards to put the foundational work in place that may be required to trigger the transformation.

Your Wake-Up Call: Three Drivers of Transformation

Set New Goals for Passion, Profit, and Growth

*Only a healthy bottom line
keeps you in business.*

Your Three Drivers of Transformation are:

1. The Passion Driver: Your Return on People

2. The Profit Driver: Your Profitable Customer Ratio

3. The Growth Driver: Leverage the Power of Whole-Brain Thinking

What could your business achieve if you could help every employee realize their capacity to help drive growth and success in your firm?

What could you accomplish if you could get inside your customers' heads and find out what they're really thinking, needing, planning, and wanting?

What would every day in your business be like if you could tap into every single scrap of talent and ingenuity your employees possess?

You're about to get three wake-up calls that will forever change the way you see your business, just as you'll always be able to see FLY instead of mysterious black shapes in the brain teaser.

Here in Part I, you'll look at Possibilities in Plain Sight with the Three Drivers of Transformation that clearly identify where you are at today, and begin to set the bar higher. Then we'll build your road map to achieve the goals you've set as you overcome five stubborn market-driven challenges with the Solutions in Plain Sight in Part II, Shift to Practicalities

Simply bringing more awareness to some things that you take for granted, and learning new ways of interpreting Possibilities currently hidden in your business with three often-overlooked Drivers of Transformation will begin the transformative process.

- The Passion Driver is your Return on People (ROP).
- The Profit Driver is your Profitable Customer Ratio.
- The Growth Driver Leverages the Power of Whole-Brain Thinking.

The Three Drivers of Transformation Are for You When ...

... you want to recapture the Passion and Purpose in your business. Earning Profit and ensuring Growth is doing a *job*. Is that enough? No!! Everyone in your organization wants to be part of doing *meaningful* work — that is, on Purpose — that protects the business and their jobs from economic turmoil while providing opportunities for themselves, their families, every employee, and their communities. Passion comes from being on Purpose and building a *legacy* — an *enduring* and highly profitable company that top talent aspires to work with and that valuable customers never want to leave; a company with Legendary Value. The first Driver, Return on People, is the key to igniting your people to be the best, letting them know where they're at today, and helping them get passionate about what they need to do to win.

... you want to earn Principled Profit. Profit earned with integrity means you're "on Purpose" and that's the most relevant measure of whether you're delivering goods and services that meet the needs of your customers in an efficient and effective way. If you're not earning all the Profit you want to today, it's simply because you're not delivering enough value or not effectively monetizing the value you create. The second Driver, your Profitable Customer Ratio, will help you change that. You'll build a strong war chest to see your company, your employees, and your customers through turbulent economic times, and you'll have the assets and the confidence to invest for growth. You'll create the ability to give back to your community and to create a legacy. With the Profitable Customer Ratio, you'll know exactly where you stand, and exactly where you need to go.

... you want sustainable Growth on Purpose: *Profitable and sustainable* Growth enables your company to invest for the future when and how you choose to do so. Purposeful Growth enables you to fulfill the responsibility of every leader to provide opportunity, not uncertainty, for every stakeholder. The third Driver, Leveraging the Power of Whole-Brain Thinking, enables you to see challenges and opportunities from a new perspective, to differentiate in uncommon ways, and to lead your market and your industry.

Ready to step up and realize your Possibilities?

How a Financial Services Firm Leveraged Passion, Profit, and Growth

A founder-led firm launched an innovative reverse mortgage product that was well-understood and popular in other areas of the world, but new to Canada.

Passion: Every person in the company was passionate about the mission to help house-rich, cash-poor seniors be able to achieve their goals and dreams, and took incredible pride in the wonderful stories shared by clients of how a reverse mortgage had improved their lives. The company had a profit-sharing model, and thus understanding Return on People and setting higher goals impacted everyone's financial abundance. Passion for the work done, and passion to be the best, drove higher levels of performance.

Profit: A lot of sweat equity and a clear understanding of what a profitable customer looked like resulted in a high level of profitability, earned with integrity. As a result, the company was able to build proprietary database technology that drove the business even more efficiently and effectively, to invest in a broader marketing campaign, and to hire top talent to expand the business.

Growth: New, smaller markets couldn't support the high-cost sales model that was used in larger markets, but the Passion within the company drove a desire to expand the service to all seniors, in all geographic locations. When staff leveraged Whole-Brain Thinking instead of "we've always done it this way," they discovered a way to partner with major financial institutions as distribution channels. Within less than a year, the company had expanded across the entire country, doubled its revenue and profit, and a lucrative IPO followed.

Your Takeaway: Profit. Passion. Growth. All within your reach, when you use your Drivers to infuse every employee as you inform, inspire, motivate, and transform.

Benchmark Your Return on People

Shatter Your Speed Limits to Achieve Extraordinary Passion, Profit, and Growth

*We overestimate what we can achieve
in 1 year and underestimate what we
can achieve in 5 years.*

What would your life be like if you could double, quadruple, or even increase your profits by a factor of 10 … safely, sustainably, and with integrity?

What would it mean to you and your family? Would you finally relax and stop working such long hours? Enjoy well-earned rewards from profit sharing or other incentives? Take the opportunity to reward good employees? Finally invest with ease in your current business or a new one? Bask in the respect from your peers and community? Have the security of knowing that you've built something extraordinary for future generations?

What would it mean to your coworkers and your community?

You may be familiar with the story of Roger Bannister, the first man to break the 4-minute mile in 1954. You probably don't know that two Swedish runners had been battling to run the mile in less than 4 minutes throughout the 1940s and had managed to shave 5 seconds off the previous world's best time, but they had not been able to break through the 4-minute psychological barrier, remaining stuck just a second and a half over it. In contrast Bannister simply decided that the 4-minute barrier *could be beaten* and did what was needed, mentally and physically, to make it happen. Just 46 days after Bannister's renowned record, John Landy broke through and bettered Bannister's record by almost half a second. When they raced against each other later that year, Bannister was the victor at 3:58.8, and his win is largely attributed to the moment when Landy looked backwards to see where Bannister was. The current men's record of 3:43.13 was set in 1999.

How often do you look *backwards* at what you accomplished last year when setting next year's goals? It's amazing what can be achieved once we focus instead on looking *forward* to what is possible, and follow the lead of those who have already achieved it.

The Passion Driver Is for You When ...

... you need to get your people onside, focused and passionate about your business;

... you need to change the mind-set in your organization to one where profits are a matter of pride to everyone; or

... you're tired of meaningless stretch goals, but still want to set the bar higher.

The second of the Three Drivers of Transformation is a key performance indicator that's rarely reported on by the business press, yet holds the key for seeing what's possible and transforming your organization: Return on People (ROP), as measured by Profit-per-Employee (P/E). I'll share data that will enable you to Benchmark against 5 years of powerful statistics to spot trends in your industry and identify Possibilities by seeing what some of the best-known companies in the world achieve. You'll learn what to do to create pride and passion in your employees by linking the statistic of Profit-per-Employee to the positive emotional impact of Return on People. Once you see the Possibilities for your firm you'll set new profitability goals and, in the challenges and solutions that follow, you'll learn how to transform *Possibilities* into *bottom-line impact.*

Tough Love: Ask Your Leadership Team Five Critical Questions

1. What is our industry standard for Return on People and where do we rank?
2. How do we know, *with certainty*, that the profits we're earning today are the optimum for our business?
3. How fully engaged are our people in behaving like owners, passionate about profit and growth?
4. Could key members of the executive team take a leave of absence, knowing with certainty that our people will step up to create all the profits we need to do everything we want to sustain and grow our business for everyone?

5. How willing are we — really — to become a John Landy or Roger Bannister and lead our industry ... or is the status quo good enough for us?

 Rapid Results Resources: Take 6 minutes to complete the "Are Your Employees Infused?" assessment at www.ProfitInPlainSight.com/Infuse and receive a customized report showing you exactly where your greatest profit opportunities lie.

Now, let's expose some common myths about profitability that keep you from seeing what's possible.

 ## Move Beyond the Myths

Which of these three myths are keeping you from realizing your Profit potential?

 ### *MYTH #1*
Margins in Our Industry Are Relatively Fixed

FACT: I hear this myth constantly. Do you? So why is it that when you look at the Profit-per-Employee metric there are clear winners whose Return on People is *substantially higher* than their closest *competitors*? They are more immune to recession and thrive even in very commoditized industries such as office supplies, insurance, chemicals, communications equipment, food and drug, machinery, and more. Will you continue to settle for *fixed* margins ... or shatter that myth?

MYTH #2
You Have to Choose Either Profit or Growth;
You Can't Have Both

FACT: Often companies that make the "fastest growing" lists are *not* profitable, which reinforces this belief. And many publications suggest that to grow quickly you have to sacrifice margins or make large investments that take years to deliver their ROI. With the Profit-per-Employee lens, it becomes clear that many of the firms leading their industries in profitability are *also* experiencing high growth rates. Large investments in people or capital are *not* required for profitable growth, as you'll see in the many examples in the Benchmarking Report I'll share with you shortly. When you think of the conversations in your company, do they focus on Profit? On Growth? Or on *profitable growth*?

MYTH #3
Revenue-per-Employee Is an Adequate Measure

FACT: When you look at almost any Top 100, Top 500 or Top 1000 list based on revenue, you'll find that one in five of those so-called "top" companies are, in fact, *losing* money! Typically, of the companies on any list who experienced revenue *increases* from the previous year, about half of them will find that profits *fell*. Gross Margin or EBITDA (Earnings Before Interest, Taxes, Depreciation, Amortization) suffer the same myopic vision and hide the truth. Measuring revenue per employee simply creates, at best, misleading information, and, at worst, a false sense of security.

If you're not consistently profitable at the very bottom of your income statement you're simply not going to stay in business. How often do you find you've increased your revenues, but there's nothing left when it comes down to the bottom line? Frustrating, isn't it?

Expand Your Thinking to Close the Gaps
Is Your Business a Couch Potato, Weekend Jogger, or World-Class Runner?

You measure ROA, ROI, ROE, and more. Why don't you measure ROP — Return on *People*? People are the most important asset, investment, and equity you have!! And when you value and engage them they're the only resource that can dynamically drive your results to new levels, in good times and in bad. Get ready to find out how to shatter your company's artificial barriers, shatter its personal best to date, and shatter the speed limits imagined by others in your industry, once you're inspired by what others have achieved.

In 2005, I started tracking Profit-per-Employee as a way to measure Return on People with data based on 72 industry categories and over 500 multinational companies. Since then, I've studied Canadian and global companies and found similar patterns. Over the past several years, some amazing results and fascinating trends have emerged. You may be surprised at what you'll learn when you benchmark your firm.

Benchmarking against some of the best companies in your industry and in the world is going to vividly change your sense of Possibilities.

Rapid Results Resources: Find out how big the gap is between where you are today and where you could be, when you download the "Profit-per-Employee Benchmarking Report" at www.ProfitInPlainSight.com/Benchmark. You'll spot trends as you look across 5 years of Profit-per-Employee data and you can get an apples-to-apples comparison with firms in your industry as well as an apples-to-oranges comparison with some of the leading companies in the world when you review all 72 different industry categories. Download it right now to get the most from the how to's that follow.

The Profit-per-Employee Benchmark

Remember your school days when teachers used to bell-curve your grades? The bell curve in Figure 1 presents the same concept, ranking publicly traded companies on a Profit-per-Employee basis to create an initial Benchmark for you.

Figure 1: BENCHMARKING YOUR RETURN ON PEOPLE[1]

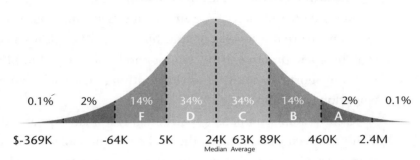

So what does the bell curve tell us about your Possibilities for Return on People?

- *Half* of the 500 companies in this benchmark earn *less than $24K* of Profit-per-Employee per year. When you think about it, that doesn't give the majority much room for investment in growth. They are some of the largest companies in the world ranked by revenue, but they are wrestling with five stubborn market-driven challenges just like you. Does that make big companies less intimidating when you think of benchmarking against them?

- The *average* company earns $63K of Profit-per-Employee (P/E) per year — a solid C, and up from $52K of P/E last year.

- The *top 2%* of companies earn an A by achieving in excess of *$460K* of Profit-per-Employee per year and many are

[1] *Results above are based on financial data reported in 2013. Download current results at www.ProfitInPlainSight.com/Benchmark.*

beloved brands. But it takes *more than five times* that to earn an A+.

- **Approximately 15% of companies in the Benchmark are *losing* money**, even though their *revenues* place them among the *largest* companies in the world and on many "top" lists.

Pause and re-read those bullet points.

Revenue-based metrics are among the most dangerous you can use to measure the success of your business, although it's a common business practice. Now, I don't know about you, but I think life's too short to work for less than nothing unless it's volunteer work done by choice!!

Clearly, some companies are leveraging human capital and the ability to execute better than others. Their talent pool finds uncommon ways to deliver value to customers and generate extraordinary results that fund ongoing growth. Isn't that exactly what solving five stubborn market-driven challenges demands?

Here are the shocking facts that solidify why this is a critical Key Performance Indicator (KPI):

- Profit-per-Employee is the best measure of how well you transform the *talents, ideas, abilities,* and *passions* of the only true source of differentiation between you and your competitors — you and your people — into *value* that customers are willing to pay for. It is your Return on People.

- The top 10% of companies earn *more than five times that of the average.* The top 1% earn *more than ten times that* of the average company. Which group would you rather be part of?

Take another pause and let those bullet points sink in.

Now, isn't running a great business all about engaging your talent to create value for customers and being rewarded for doing so?

Figure 2: WHICH FIRM DO YOU WANT TO BE?

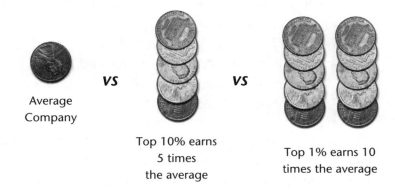

Average
Company

vs

Top 10% earns
5 times
the average

vs

Top 1% earns 10
times the average

Your first reaction to your Benchmarking results may be, "But I'm not a big, multinational company" or "Our tax rates are different" or "It's the exchange rate differences" or "Bottom-line profits can be manipulated, top-line revenue is a safer measurement." I hear all of these reactions frequently and most of those leaders, although they're doing a lot of right things, usually find that their company earns substantially *less* Profit-per-Employee than the average company. They're usually a D — or even an F.

Since you're in the section of *seeing Possibilities* so that you can escape "we've always done it this way," I'm going to invite you to keep an open mind on this. I'll show you why the statistics I'm giving you are relevant, regardless of how big or small your company is today or in which country your firm is headquartered.

If you have an accounting background, you're probably thinking of all the ways companies work to minimize net profit by legally manipulating various charges to achieve a tax-friendly bottom line. Please set that aside for the moment because when all companies are doing so and doing so consistently, it becomes irrelevant for the purposes of this Benchmark. The Profit-Per-Employee Key Performance Indicator (KPI) is not designed to be a precise financial methodology, but merely a tool to see greater Possibilities. As with all KPIs, it has both benefits and drawbacks, which are fully outlined in the Report you downloaded. You did download it, didn't you?

 GAP #1

Many Firms Experienced 100% Increases in Profit-per-Employee Per Year in the 5-Year Period Bracketing the 2008 Recession

Did you? If not, you've got a gap between your Possibilities and your current state. The data shows that they *didn't* do it by downsizing. Unfortunately, that is the quickest but most shortsighted and damaging way to increase your Profit-per-Employee ratio. Instead, they found creative approaches for leveraging the talent within their organization to create value for customers. In fact, top-performing companies *increased* their number of employees during the 2006-2011 recessionary period. Wouldn't it be nice never to have to look a good employee in the eye again and tell them that their job has disappeared ... or have the resources to hire all the talent you need?

A common question is, "But doesn't the industry you're in make a difference?" Yes, but not as much as you would think. Some industries are generally more profitable than others (not *every* industry can attain $623K of Profit-per-Employee!), but when you look at the details in the Benchmarking Report (see Rapid Results Resources earlier in this section) you'll see many industry categories include firms earning an A, B, C, D and F. Although they are in the same industry, they are performing at *very* different levels.

In every industry there is usually one firm that consistently outperforms all the others on the Profit-per-Employee metric. They simply leverage the talent they have better than anyone else to create value for customers that earns Profit with integrity. Shouldn't that firm be yours?

Here's a Whole New Meaning to Follow the Leader

When I ask executive mentoring groups to share their Profit-per-Employee results in a round table environment, there are inevitably a few in the negative ranks, several clustered at the low end of the bell curve, and one or two doing substantially better than everyone else. The shift in mind-set is immediate. Every one of the executives wants to know what the successful group members are doing, and they want to be the ones with the bragging rights.

Your Takeaway: The scenery only changes for the lead sled dog. The fastest way to ignite pride and passion is to see someone else in the lead and decide to achieve more.

GAP #2
Over Time Opportunities to Profit With Integrity Get Lost in Business as Usual

Costs have a way of working their way into the system, even good initiatives become outdated and market opportunities shift. You may be wrestling right now with low margins in highly commoditized markets, with no road map to address profit shortfalls with confidence. Yet seemingly minor opportunities to improve revenues, uncover new growth opportunities, and reduce costs across a customer base can add up to big profits, especially in low-margin industries. Reframing what is possible based on Profit-per-Employee holds the key.

A poll of over 1000 business owners, leaders, and key managers shows most are seeking to increase profits by 10-25% within 3-5 years until they see their greater Possibilities through the lens of the Profit-per-Employee Benchmark. Then a seismic shift occurs.

They are shocked to find that in settling for incrementalism, they're being left behind by others who are achieving those goals *every year*.

The Norm Is the Problem

When management groups are asked, "What would the rest of your team describe as a reasonable goal for increasing profits," the answers almost always come back in the single digits. It's an answer they're not happy with because it's below their own expectations, but it's an answer we've all learned to accept as the norm.

Our Takeaway: Use the Benchmark as a tool to break out of complacency.

GAP #3

You May Be Dismayed to Learn that Your Company Doesn't Compare Very Well Against the Benchmark

Many business leaders initially find that their "grade" does not reflect all the time, energy, money, and sacrifices they've sunk into their business, and you may initially find this too. The Benchmark becomes a Driver of Transformation when implemented well, and the good news is that the wake-up call to your Possibilities is only the first step — knowing where you rank is a powerful motivator. Part II, Shift to Practicalities, will show you how to turn wherever you are today into a top-performing score.

From a Dry Diaper to a Cold, Wet One

When a group of individual contributors, managers, and senior leaders in a 50 Best Managed company (with a profit sharing plan) gathered around the boardroom table to kick off their Profit in Plain Sight road map, they were asked where they thought they ranked on the Profit-per-Employee bell curve. The typical answer was a C.

You could have heard a pin drop when it was revealed that they were a D- and that some of their competitors were doing better. Then the buzz started. With a noticeable level of enthusiasm, they wanted to know "how do we get to be an A+." The comfortable, dry diaper that they'd all been used to had suddenly become cold and wet ... and they wanted to change it. That's passion that moves the needle.

Your Takeaway: Buy-in is immediate once people see Possibilities and want to be the best.

 Rapid Results Resources: Don't have your copy of the "Profit-per-Employee Benchmarking Report" yet? There's only one way to know where you stand, how big the gap is, and where you can go. Download your Report and take 30 minutes to read it and Benchmark your firm right now: www.ProfitInPlainSight.com/Benchmark.

Perhaps you're already outperforming your industry. If so, set your sights higher, against the overall Benchmark. There are many B, A and even A+ Roger Bannisters and John Landys that you can be inspired by and learn from.

Many leaders polled say they are only *somewhat* confident that they have the skills and abilities within their company to achieve the level of profitability they *need*, let alone the one that they *want*. All of them agree that sooner would be better. There's a gap and they don't know how to close it. So they settle for less.

Consequences:
Lost Dreams Due to Business as Usual

Unless you know how well you *could* be doing, how do you know with certainty how well you *should* be doing? Not knowing is simply foolish.

Taking action to Benchmark and set the bar higher might seem like a "nice to do" and who's got time for that? *You* do, if you have time for e-mail every day. Every year that you settle for achieving less than you could costs your company opportunities that you can't regain. You can't afford *not* to achieve your full potential, because your competitors will leave you in the dust.

Without exception, every business leader I've spoken with has identified investments in their business that are either on hold due to lack of profitability or which could be achieved more easily with a better bottom line and a stronger balance sheet. Take a moment to study the What's on Hold Checklist (see Figure 3) and fix in your own mind what business as usual is costing you in the way of missed opportunities.

Figure 3: **OUR BUCKET LIST: WHAT'S ON HOLD BECAUSE WE NEED MORE PROFIT?**

Our current profits are preventing us from being able to: *(check all that apply)*	**With a "Sky's the Limit" bottom line and a stronger balance sheet we would:** *(check all that apply)*
☐ Invest in new equipment	☐ Invest in new equipment
☐ Reduce debt	☐ Reduce debt
☐ Hire more talented people	☐ Hire more talented people
☐ Invest in/acquire new facilities	☐ Invest in/acquire new facilities
☐ Fund acquisitions	☐ Fund acquisitions
☐ Become fully automated	☐ Become fully automated
☐ Expand into new business sectors/locations	☐ Expand into new business sectors/locations
☐ Increase capacity	☐ Increase capacity
☐ Give raises to good people	☐ Give raises to good people
☐ Implement meaningful profit sharing	☐ Implement meaningful profit sharing
☐ Do more marketing	☐ Do more marketing
☐ Invest in training	☐ Invest in training
☐ Invest in technology	☐ Invest in technology
☐ Buy back shares	☐ Buy back shares
☐ Position for a liquidity event/ buy out	☐ Position for a liquidity event/ buy out
☐ Sleep more soundly	☐ Sleep more soundly
☐ Other: _____	☐ Other: _____
On a scale of 1-10, how badly do I want us to recapture these lost opportunities? _____	On a scale of 1-10, how badly do I want these change-the-playing-field opportunities for us? _____

Think carefully before you answer those two final questions. Taking action on Passion, Profit, and Growth isn't for everyone. Do you want it badly enough to do something about it, or is it simply a "nice to do"? Without a strong desire to achieve one or the other or *both* lists, I can't help you.

But if you are willing to commit to going beyond business as usual and making your list happen in less time than you're spending on e-mail today, I can.

Are you highly confident that you'll get there with what you're doing today?

My goals are two-fold: to get you to expand your sense of Possibilities by setting new goals and to help you become *highly* confident in reaching those goals.

The confidence to achieve extraordinary goals is what you can achieve with the proven strategies and tactics included in this book and with the resources that accompany it.

I Didn't Know I Couldn't

In my very first job out of university, I turned an industry-standard 40% discount into an average discount of less than 5% in a highly competitive industry where everyone was scrambling to come in with the lowest price. I was selling business forms back in the carbon and carbonless days, and I simply asked two questions: Show me a completed form, and show me where each part ends up going. I almost always found waste and I was almost always able to recommend a smaller form with fewer copies.

I could quote list prices and eliminate discounts because I'd changed the playing field. It was simply a matter of taking the time to have a Value Creation Conversation with my customers, while most of my competitors simply asked if they could quote on what already existed. My customers benefited, my company benefited, and I benefited — just by selling *value*, not price. I was able to do it primarily because I didn't know that I *couldn't*. I was young, enthusiastic, and since my commissions were inversely tied to my discounts, I was motivated to figure it out!

Remember the early days of your career when anything was possible? How would it feel to go there again? Just imagine how quickly you could make the investments you want to make in your business if you could put that type of extra money on your bottom line, just by focusing on what you *can* do in your business, not what you *can't* do because of those crazy things called industry norms. It's those kinds of successes over the years that have been captured with *how to's* in the Solutions in Plain Sight that follow.

Your Takeaway: Dialogue with your customers is key to changing the playing field and achieving what is really possible.

There are couch potatoes and world-class runners and we usually associate couch potatoes with underperformers who watch too much TV. That doesn't apply to you, but as a useful motivator, try this. Whenever you sit down to flick on the news, a show, or sports, I want you to ask yourself if your company is a sluggish couch potato, a weekend jogger, or a world-class runner when it comes to your Return on People. Then, decide which one you want to be.

Solutions in Plain Sight
Ignite the Passion and Pride to Be World Class

By the way, do you know what triggered Roger Bannister to go beyond performing the way he and others always had? He never won an Olympic medal. In fact, he came fourth in the Helsinki Olympics in 1952 and acknowledged that had he won, he would probably have retired and would never have run the mile in less than 4 minutes in 1954. Instead, it took being disappointed in his level of achievement compared to others, setting a clear goal, some hard training, and a competitive spirit to reach a breakthrough.

Hmmm, that sounds a lot like what Benchmarking your Return on People can do for you, doesn't it? Nobody remembers who won Olympic Gold in 1952. But we all remember Roger Bannister's 4-minute mile.

So I want you to delve into the report you downloaded and look at the goals that others have already reached as outlined — overall and in your industry. And then I want you to focus on shattering your speed limits on profitability.

However, if you decide you want to settle for life in the slow lane or rest on your laurels do yourself a favor. Close this book, pay it forward to someone else, and return to business as usual.

SOLUTION IN PLAIN SIGHT #1
Your Wake-Up Call for Passion, Profit, and Growth

Take a moment right now to calculate your current Profit-per-Employee (see Figure 4) based on information from your most recent Annual Income Statement, so that you can do a preliminary Benchmark. Make sure you use the absolute bottom-line number, Net Income, and not an interim measure such as Gross Margin or EBITDA. For your employee number, use Full-Time-Equivalent (FTE) numbers if you need to, but do not include contractors or other outsourced resources — for purposes of this exercise, you don't need to be exact. If you don't have access to this information, go ahead and skip ahead to Solutions in Plain Sight #2 where you'll plot your industry information, and simply evaluate how various firms in your industry are performing.

Figure 4: **CALCULATE YOUR RETURN ON PEOPLE**

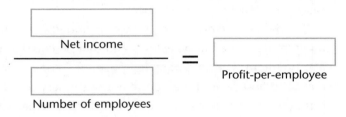

RETURN ON PEOPLE

Seeing What's Possible...

Write down your Net Income ÷ Number of Employees

$$\frac{\text{Net income}}{\text{Number of employees}} = \boxed{\qquad} \text{ Profit-per-employee}$$

**How do you KNOW, with certainty,
if it's a "good" result for your business?**

_____

_____

One of the challenges for some leaders is that they unintentionally "game" the metric. That is, they use various income numbers that are above the absolute bottom line or they round down the numbers of staff, especially if they're a seasonal business. Do yourself the courtesy of making this real. The Benchmark is based on the bottom-line income that publicly traded companies report in their financials and the employee numbers are based on their reported head count.

Plot your Profit-per-Employee result on the worksheet in the Benchmark Report you downloaded. What's your grade? Does it feel like the grade you want to earn, based on how hard you work in your business and how much value you deliver to customers? When you see what others have achieved, do you see Possibilities to improve it? Even if it's bad news it's better than not knowing, because now you can take steps to change the status quo.

This Wake-Up Call Delivered Results

One CEO in the retail electronics industry shifted his expectations from "maintaining where we're at today" to "a profit increase of 25% in the next year" immediately after Benchmarking himself on the bell curve.

He then got very clear on where he added value that was different from the big box stores and that he could price for at a premium, selectively applied price-for-value actions, identified and cleared the sludge out of the service side of his business, and implemented several of the 5Rs of proactive customer profitability management (you'll learn about these in a later section).

He achieved the goal he never thought he could despite being in a highly competitive industry. His business went from struggling to thriving.

Your Takeaway: Take the time to Benchmark and get a wake-up call that will be well worth the effort!

 ## SOLUTION IN PLAIN SIGHT #2
Benchmark Against Your Industry

Your next step is to Benchmark against your own industry, to deepen your insights on your current performance and Possibilities. The Benchmarking Report includes 5 years of data across 72 different industry categories, and you'll be able to find industry names that you recognize. Go ahead and plot your industry's results on the bell curve worksheet in the report. Do you have some catching up to do or are you already performing at a higher level than your industry?

I often see leaders slip back into complacency if they find they're no worse than their industry. That is not the point here. Your entire *industry* may be settling for less as a couch potato or a weekend jogger. If you want to achieve the investments in your business that you checked off on the "Sky's the Limit" list, you'll want you to be Roger Bannister or John Landy.

The Good News If You're Not a Huge Multinational

The good news is that you have an advantage if you're smaller and more nimble than the companies in this Benchmark. You will see a notable shift in your Profit-per-Employee results more quickly and easily, once you implement the near-term Solutions in Plain Sight in Part II, Shift to Practicalities.

Understanding Your Value Add Holds the Key

Nine out of ten leaders and their teams with revenues of $15-$250M find their grade to be a C or lower when they first Benchmark. Of those who fully implement the systematic Profit in Plain Sight Framework, more than 80% shift to a higher grade within a year. How?

They fully engage their teams in hearing the voice of the customer and responding in value-add ways. You'll learn those exact steps to listen in new ways and respond in ways that add value as you work through the material that follows.

Your Takeaway: When Benchmark results are shared broadly among all employees, the outcome is the information, inspiration, and motivation to transform today's bottom line into industry-leading results that reflect how much value you add to your customers.

Leave behind whether you're a D, a C or a B. This is not about judging you or about saying that you're not doing the right things. After all, you've never had a tool before that shows you what is possible. This is about creating the outcomes you want by doing *more things right* to find the profits you need to fund your business bucket list and achieve the business goals that you've set.

Calculate the Profit-per-Employee that you'll need to achieve everything you checked off on that "Sky's the Limit" bucket list earlier. Ballpark it if you need to. For now, just mentally increase your net profit to the number you really want and *use the exact same number of employees as you did before to calculate your new Profit-per-Employee*. Do this exercise even if you don't have access to your current financials.

Leaders at all levels of the organization often give me the "yeah, right" look when asked to use the same number of employees to achieve much higher profit goals. Many of the Solutions in Plain Sight throughout this book and the 57 Accelerators in the systematic Profit in Plain Sight Framework *leverage* the resources you already have. As you pursue some of the more advanced aspects, it's likely that growing your top and bottom lines will require more staff. When you implement the Profit-per-Employee metric as a KPI, you'll update your employee numbers as you go. First, let's see where you want to be with the talent you've already got. Humor me. Use the same number of employees this time around.

Profits Skyrocketed with NO Increase in Employees

Here's how a small regional player in the financial services industry transformed into a publicly traded national company with twice the revenue and three times the profit, all without adding more staff.

We just needed to shake up the business model a bit to do it. Instead of relying on a conventional high-cost personal selling model with an "over the kitchen table" conversation, they formed alliances with major non-competing financial institutions where the end clients already had access to a trusted advisor. The advisor facilitated a sales teleconference between the client and an expert in a call center, and then simply processed the paperwork.

What would often take two hours of travel and selling time was reduced to approximately half an hour, and enabled the regional player to expand into smaller markets where a conventional sales model would have been prohibitively expensive.

Your Takeaway: You don't always need more people when you can impact profitability with productivity. You may just need to trigger more value from the talent you already have!

Plot your new number on the worksheet in the Benchmark Report. Does that now feel doable and achievable based on seeing how other companies in your industry, and beyond, have already shattered the conventional standards that your competitors are settling for? If this has inspired you to reach a higher goal, then we've achieved our first objective. You should have a bell curve that looks something like the one in Figure 5, where X is your Profit-per-Employee today, Y represents your competitors and Z is the Profit-per-Employee you require to fulfill the items on your checklist.

Figure 5: **YOUR NEW BELL CURVE**

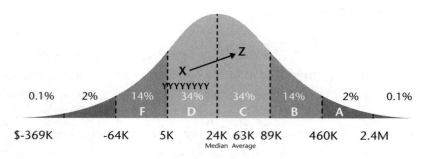

Organizations often find that they're currently at a D or a C and simply need to improve *within* a grade level or possibly move *one grade* higher to achieve their blue-sky profit goal and bucket list. We all used to be able to do that in school when we had to, didn't we? But it meant we needed to study harder, get some help, or even hire a tutor.

 Rapid Results Resources: Access free resources to help and even get "tutoring" at www.ProfitInPlainSight.com/ProfitU.

Use the Comprehensive Resources —
Never Reinvent the Wheel

Your path to Passion, Profit, and Growth is to share your Return on People information broadly across your organization. If only the executive team sees the gap and the Possibilities, then you've missed out on your most powerful opportunity to ignite pride in your organization — getting your people to want to lead the charge. Your people know they're good. They want to be the best. They will help you close the gap if you show them what "best" is and ask for their help to get there. When you show them what "best" is, that will ignite their passion to make it happen.

One of the biggest problems leaders and managers who want to implement the Profit-per-Employee metric across their organization experience is that their initial thinking trends to frequent measurement, breaking it down by department, and using it to drive incentive programs. This is exactly the *wrong* way to implement this.

I also see leaders who are uncomfortable with sharing Profit-per-Employee data with their employees, especially if they're highly profitable or where unions are involved, due to the fear of triggering the "where's my share" question. Many of the most successful organizations have profit sharing plans that are completely transparent, but if that's not in your comfort zone, simply share the bell curve in Figure 5 without the numbers and ask for their help to make the shift to a better grade.

 Rapid Results Resources: There are straightforward ways to avoid these issues and implement for impact. When you're ready to implement this powerful KPI to create pride and passion in your organization, download specific considerations and recommendations for how to do it the right way with the Return on People Implementation Resources at www.ProfitInPlainSight.com/ ImplementROP.

The other big challenge for leaders and their teams who get inspired by the Possibilities they see here is that they try to achieve their goals using the same tired approaches they've used in the past. Cutting costs and discretionary spending. Discounting to drive revenues. Delaying good hires.

Stop! This is about transformation and you can't shrink your way to Passion, Profit, and Growth. You want to break free of the "we've always done it this way" mentality and finally transform market-related challenges with the uncommon approaches of the Solutions in Plain Sight road map in Part II, Shift to Practicalities.

You'll be pleasantly surprised by the amount of time you need to commit to really see impact on your bottom line — the owners, leaders, managers, supervisors, and individual contributors I work with find it to be *less* than the 1-2 hours they're currently spending daily on e-mail. What if key members of your team and your entire organization committed to focus just as much time on bottom-line Passion, Profit, and Growth as they do on e-mail?

Do you think you'll start to shatter some speed limits and move the needle in your business pretty quickly? Absolutely!

Set Goals; Get Results

An executive in the specialty chemicals industry who saw this information in a seminar immediately said, "We've been setting our goals too low."

He had been willing to settle for $7K of Profit-per-Employee and realized just how much more potential he had, once he Benchmarked on the bell curve. He set a higher goal of $25K.

His team used the Rapid Results Resources to achieve it in less than 1 year, in less time than they were spending on e-mail.

Your Takeaway: Don't settle for being less than the best.

Summary

Knowledge of what is and what could be is priceless. Without it, you're like a ship without a rudder, simply drifting with the tide instead of moving purposefully toward your destination. You waste a lot of time negotiating the numbers based on past performance, instead of simply saying, "Let's set the bar higher and build a plan to get there," and then fully engaging the passion your people can bring to the table to help you. Otherwise, you're leaving money on the table that should be yours and there will never be enough on the bottom line to make all the investments required to secure the future of your business in turbulent economic times and in a changing global economy. Your people feel at risk rather than part of the solution. Playing it safe with incremental increases is anything but.

As with all things in business, Benchmarking your Profit-per-Employee to ignite the power of Return on People and taking responsibility to strengthen your bottom line so that it reflects a job well done is an ongoing process. It's the second of the Three Drivers of Transformation I promised you, and it's just a starting point.

You can spend a lot of time to figure out how to improve profitability on your own or you can use proven approaches that deliver results.

You've learned that Profit-per-Employee is the best measure of how well you're transforming *talent* into *value* that customers are willing to buy. With the downloadable Report, you now have the information you need to Benchmark against your own industry and against revered global leaders, to change your perceptions in the blink of an eye and to set and achieve extraordinary Profits by shattering your speed limits on profitability. Without Benchmarking you will stay tethered, resigned to business as usual.

This isn't a "nice to do" for "someday." You want to take action on this immediately, not only to satisfy your curiosity, but simply because it will quickly and easily enable you to set the bar so much higher. Every time you watch TV, you get to decide if couch potato or world-class runner is where you want to be in your business.

When you measure, benchmark, infuse your team, set new goals, and follow a tried and true plan to achieve them, you have the potential and the means to lead your industry. You can follow in the footsteps of those whose achievements in other industries inspire you and build a company that will change your life and the lives of those around you, starting with your people. They'll appreciate it!

Only 1% of leaders ever take action on what they've committed to do. Those are the 1% who are earning above-average grades on the Profit-per-Employee Benchmark. Throughout the book you'll find Action Plans to help you implement the Three Solutions in Plain Sight that every Challenge includes. You'll easily set the bar higher and engage your people in helping you get there. And that's tough for your competitors to beat.

This works. You can do it. You will succeed.

Take these Actions

Transformation takes more than awareness and good intentions.

Assessment	1. Take 6 minutes to complete the "Are Your People Infused?" assessment at *www.ProfitInPlainSight.com/Infuse*, and send the link to your team so that you can compare notes.
Resource	2. Download the "Profit-per-Employee Benchmarking Report" at *www.ProfitInPlainSight.com/Benchmark* to take action on the three Solutions in Plain Sight.
Action Item	3. Schedule a team meeting to: • Ask the Tough Love questions from the beginning of this Chapter. • Compare notes from the Infuse assessment with your team. • Get a very clear picture of what you're putting on hold and what that is costing your business, so that you can use the systematic Profit in Plain Sight Framework to achieve it. Shatter your speed limits by setting a goal that will really enable you to achieve your Sky's the Limit list for your business. • Commit to implement the Profit-per-Employee KPI as a catalyst to ignite pride and passion with your employees using the Profit-per-Employee Implementation Resources at *www.ProfitInPlainSight.com/ImplementROP*.

Small Steps. Big Impact!

Five Minutes, Five Questions:
Reflect for Deeper Learning

Your first step is *internal* transformation, to identify what attitudes have already shifted and what behaviors will follow.

1. How have my speed limits been shattered as a result of Bench-marking our firm on the basis of Profit-per-Employee?

   _____

2. What would the type of Sky's the Limit increase that I've calculated mean for our business?

   _____

3. What resistance am I feeling at the moment? Do those concerns hold true as I examine them or do they simply reflect patterns of thinking that are keeping us stuck?

   _____

   _____

4. What resistance do I anticipate from my team to setting goals that shatter our speed limits? How will I open their minds and help them reset their expectations without having to shoulder the entire load myself?

   _____

5. How genuinely committed am I to achieving the new profitability goals that will enable us to make investments in our business and what is the upside if I do? What is the downside if we remain stuck in business as usual?

   _____

Inform. Inspire. Motivate. Transform.
Infuse. Enthuse.

Increase Your Profitable Customer Ratio

Eliminate the Everyday Business Mistake that's Costing You Millions

Only customers create cash flow.

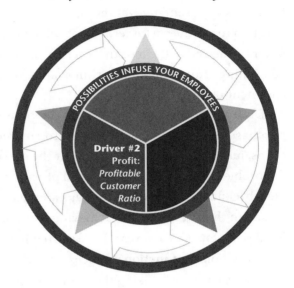

What would it be like if you could do business only with highly profitable customers who value their relationship with you?

How relieved would you be if you could eliminate the problems caused by the customers who are costing you more than they're worth ... without taking a huge hit to your volume or bottom line?

What would be possible in your business if you could achieve "the nirvana" of profitable growth — doing more business, with more customers, at higher prices?

In the 1990s Digital Equipment (DEC), once the world's second-largest computer company, downsized to virtually nothing and was absorbed into a company that true "Deccies" never even saw as a competitor. It happened because of one common business mistake that you're probably making too.

Digital incented and compensated on *revenue*, which provoked some very aberrant behavior. Sales managers would tag along with their sales representatives at the end of every quarter with only one question to ask the customer, "What will it take to get the purchase order by the end of the month?" thereby undoing months of value-add selling efforts and diminishing value to the level of bargain-basement pricing. Sound familiar?

Digital inadvertently *trained* its customers to schedule their purchases so that DEC would agree to any requested pricing or terms, just to "make the numbers." At the end of every fiscal year, the problem got worse. Reps booked phantom orders that conveniently cancelled as soon as the reps and managers had officially locked in their rewards for "achieving" their budget and the new fiscal year started. Each year, DEC started in the hole on revenues and the whole dysfunctional process started again.

Sure, they were "making the numbers" on paper, but to a large extent it wasn't *profitable business*. While there were also technology and marketing issues, it's notable that Digital was still rewarding successful sales representatives with trips to Hawaii as the company bled to death and downsized almost 120,000 employees worldwide. They got what they measured. They got what they incented. And their focus on revenue instead of profit contributed to the downfall of a once-great company.

Digital's death throes underscored that revenue and profit are two very different things and at the end of the day only a healthy bottom line keeps you in business and able to provide secure employment, be an indispensable resource that your customers can count on, and give back to your community.

Too many businesses focus on measuring and rewarding *revenue* or *gross margin*. Those measures are among the most common yet most dangerous business practices that we all take for granted, and there's a better way.

The Profit Driver Is for You When ...

... you're sick and tired of generating top-line growth, but never seeing it translate into money you can take to the bank;

... you know you're losing money on some of your customers, but haven't found an effective way to stop the bleeding; or

... you struggle to get your customer-facing people to understand how their everyday actions are creating or destroying profitability.

Want to put some Passion, Profit, and Growth in your business? First I'll introduce you to the *easier* way to get the customer profitability information you require to make good decisions *without* complicated and time-consuming accounting practices that provide exact data too late to act upon. Instead, you'll take a *good-is-good-enough-right-now* approach to get meaningful information and determine the best strategic and tactical profitability actions. And you and your team will have some fun doing it, especially when you see it delivering results in less than 30 days.

Next I'll share the innovative three-part Customer Profitability Diamond that reveals the significant profit opportunities *already* in your business and exposes the profit leaks that you need to close, without having to make the large investments in people or capital that typically drive growth at the *expense* of profits.

And finally we'll use the Customer Profitability Diamond to reveal your Profitable Customer Ratio — the catalyst that will *really* shift the needle on profitability in your business. We'll tackle each of these opportunities with Action Plans in subsequent Challenges.

Note: If you already measure net profit by customer on an adjusted cost basis or similar accounting-based method, you will still get value from the process I'm about to outline, because there's a qualitative side to customer profitability that impacts your business and your bottom line in ways that accounting measures can't track. If you measure gross margin, I will show you how to uncover the hidden gotchas in that method.

Tough Love: Ask Your Leadership Team Five Critical Questions

1. Which can we name more easily: a list of our *biggest* customers based on revenue or a list of our *most profitable* customers?

2. How often are we putting up with customers we know are costing us money because we don't have a better alternative to restore them to profitability, or because we need the volume to support fixed costs?

3. How often do we find ourselves between a rock and a hard place trying to cut the cost of sales or cut the costs of service ... without really understanding how those decisions will impact our customer relationships?

4. What's our customer retention plan beyond sales calls, lunches, golf and event tickets? Are we passionate about retaining our best clients, or simply ho-hum?

5. Do we focus primarily on getting *new* business or do we creatively uncover new ways to do *more* business with our current customers?

Rapid Results Resources: Take 6 minutes to complete the "Are Your Customers Enthused?" assessment at www.ProfitInPlainSight.com/Enthuse and receive a customized report showing you exactly where your critical profit leaks and greatest profit opportunities lie.

 ## Move Beyond the Myths

Which of these three myths are keeping you from doing the right thing for your business and your customers?

 ### MYTH #1
Customer Profitability Is Too Difficult to Measure

FACT: By traditional accounting standards, yes it is. Most businesses cannot afford the time or expense to develop the types of complex accounting systems that allocate costs and attempt to calculate profit per customer. However, when you take a *qualitative* approach, customer profitability rankings for your 100 biggest revenue accounts can be established in less than an afternoon. With that information, you will drive good decision making and decisive action.

 ### MYTH #2
Gross Margin Is an Adequate Measure of Customer Profitability

FACT: Gross margin is a great start compared to the pure "revenue" view taken by many companies. However, many of the variable costs to serve that customer, from the time they become aware of your company to the time they buy, use, and dispose of your product, lie below the gross margin line and must be factored in. Many *hidden costs*, such as the impact of an abusive customer on morale, can never be captured by conventional accounting methods, yet still impact profitability.

MYTH #3
When Top-line Growth Is a Priority, Profitability Is Less Important

On the contrary. Top line growth is only of value when it delivers *profitable* growth. Yes, increasing volume can help spread fixed costs more broadly, with positive impact on profitability. More often, additional revenue on the top line simply leaks out *below* the gross margin level, leaving little for the bottom line. Managers often say that they're focused on top-line growth so they really don't look at profitability. A common argument is "we need the volume," with the implication that volume at any cost is a good thing. Growth and profitability need to go hand in hand.

Expand Your Thinking to Close the Gaps
Get out of the Revenue Trap

Leaders frequently confess that they can't easily measure profit by customer or that they don't get beyond gross margin per customer. They find that not having the information to make good decisions becomes their first obstacle to Passion, Profit, and Growth. Others admit that they know who is profitable and who is not, but they haven't found an effective way to deal with the customers who are costing them their profits.

In the first Driver (Return on People), you saw a great example of how easily we all take the dangerous revenue metric for granted (as noted the Benchmarking Report was derived from a Top 500 listing based on *revenue*). Many of these companies are held up as shining examples in the press because they're *big*, but when you look at them on the basis of profitability, almost one in five is losing money ... and some of them are losing a *lot* of money. They are far from being top companies, yet the myth of revenue-based rankings continues.

Too many companies default to focusing on revenue because they can track changes month to month. That's fine as a starting point as an easy and accurate measure, less subject to manipulation. Just don't make the mistake of thinking that growing revenues are predictive of growing profits until you use the Solutions in Part II to ensure that it's profitable revenue.

The High Costs of Focusing on Revenue

As you saw in the Digital Equipment example, revenue wasn't being accounted for accurately due to the phantom orders and was actually a predictor of *unprofitable* growth. Imagine the internal costs of undoing all those orders and revising production schedules and forecasts when they were cancelled — the problems driven by a focus on revenue simply kept compounding themselves.

Your Takeaway: If you measure Revenue, you get Revenue. If you measure Profit, you get Profit.

GAP #2
Profit Leaks Go Unnoticed When You're in the Revenue Trap

Over and over, mystified business owners tell me they don't see any increased bottom-line return even when they have a great year on the top line. Does this look familiar? (See Figure 1.)

Figure 1: **BOTTOM VERSUS TOP LINE**

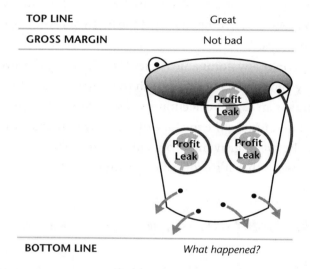

TOP LINE	Great
GROSS MARGIN	Not bad
BOTTOM LINE	*What happened?*

If you've ever had a great year on the top line but had very little to show for it on the bottom line, then you know about profitability leaks. There are dozens of them, and it is surprisingly easy to plug them and achieve better bottom-line results. Gross margin may help spot the customers who grind for discounts, but it does not address all the leaks that happen below that line (see Figure 2).

Figure 2: WHERE ARE YOU LEAKING PROFITS?

	Revenue Measures Fail to Capture Leaks	Gross Margin Measures Capture Tip-of-the-Iceberg Profit Leaks	Profit Measures Capture Every Profit Leak
Revenue			
Cost of Goods Sold	✗		✓
R & D	✗	✗	✓
Selling, General, and Admin Expenses	✗	✗	✓
Non-recurring Expenses	✗	✗	✓
Interest and Income Tax	✗	✗	✓
Extraordinary Items	✗	✗	✓

It's the profit leaks that destroy your bottom line, even in a good year.

As a colleague says, "Measuring revenue is vanity. Measuring profit is sanity."

Over-servicing, providing special terms, excessive re-works, special requests, change orders or kowtowing to high-maintenance customers are just a few of the leaks that hit your bottom line. If you've ever lost a good employee who just couldn't take the customer complaints or abuse any longer, you know that you incurred a huge cost to your business that a gross margin focus will never capture.

Yet all of those leaks can be plugged when you turn a spotlight on your Profitable Customer Ratio. As long as you're in the dark with no visibility, you'll keep losing money on unprofitable customers and losing opportunities for profit and growth with the rest of your customer base.

The Costly Mistake of the Peanut Butter Approach

One general manager started to laugh ruefully when the diagram of profit leaks was shown in a seminar.

He confessed that he'd inherited a sales team of "good ol' boys" who had their favorite customers ... and favorite golf courses. Each year, the long-term customers would be wined and dined, regardless of how much business they were doing, because it was "important to maintain the relationship."

Yes, relationships are important, but investing in an account using "we've always done it this way" approaches rather than determining whether to invest in sales, invest in service, and invest in both at a level proportional to the account's business is one of the most common profit leaks I see.

Your Takeaway: Match your sales and service investments to the value and potential of the account.

 GAP #3
Accounting-based Approaches Are Not the Answer

Those who've tried to implement accounting-driven approaches to measure profit per customer often report that they've ended up with expensive, time-consuming, complex accounting systems that either fail to deliver any relevant information or that deliver precise data, but no insights for managerial decision-making. Many default to measuring just revenue per customer which causes faulty decision-making on how much can be invested in the relationship.

Almost every customer starts out profitable, unless you're using a loss-leader strategy, but many don't stay that way. Being able to implement different profitability strategies for those who are profitable versus those who aren't is critical for realizing Passion, Profit, and Growth.

Still a Black Hole, Despite Millions Spent

One manager in an engineering firm confessed that they had been building an accounting-based system for *over 3 years* and still couldn't get meaningful data on profitability, despite investing well over $1M.

Imagine if they'd taken the easier approach to getting "good is good enough for good decision-making" and spent that million to add value for their customers!

Your Takeaway: Good-is-good-enough-for-good-decision-making is more profitable than perfection.

Consequences
The Sky-High Costs of Business as Usual

Taking action to figure out customer profitability might seem like a "nice to do" and who's got time for that? *You* do, if you have enough time for e-mail. Every unprofitable customer is a leak that requires you to essentially write a check to them that could be better spent on your own business.

Does the 80-20 Rule Hold True on Customer Profitability?

A lab supply company thought they had healthy, growing revenues, but they found they were losing money on an astonishing *33%* of their customers and *40%* of their product lines! On the customer side, it was the equivalent of writing a check for $200,000 *every month* to those customers. On the product side, they might just as well have carried a pile of $1000 bills into their R&D lab each month and burned them.

They got a wake-up call they couldn't ignore and they're not alone. Many companies find that the 80-20 rule holds true on customer profitability. About 20% of all your customers are generating almost all the profits, but it's probably *not* the large-revenue customers that are top of mind. Unfortunately the bottom 20% often cost you an amount *equal* to those profits and some of them may be your nightmare customers; others may be unprofitable in more subtle ways. Those customers who are between the two extremes can often be your biggest challenge and your biggest opportunity, because they're your biggest group of customers and they're often below your radar.

You can't afford not to get the kind of transformational wake-up call that the lab company did, especially if you have the same sort of surprises lurking in your business ... and you probably do.

Your Takeaway: Leverage the 80-20 rule to your best advantage when moving the needle on profitability.

We all know how annoying a leaky tap can be. I want you hearing that slow, steady drip, drip, drip in your head until you take action. You're reading this book because you want to transform your business.

All you require is the right systematic approach to achieve that so — let's jump right in.

Solutions in Plain Sight
Shine the Spotlight on Your Profitable Customer Ratio

Leaders and managers polled at all levels in the organization say they know who their big customers are and they spend extra time with them. That's the proof that they've fallen into the Revenue Trap and as a result they're stuck going in circles with five stubborn market-driven challenges because they don't have the insights they need to transform them into Passion, Profit, and Growth.

There's a critical foundation element you want to have in place before you can implement the Solutions in Plain Sight throughout this book — the deceptively simple but very powerful Who's Who of your Customer Profitability Diamond.

First you'll learn what insights the Diamond offers and then you'll learn what to do with this tool to transform your business.

For clarity and brevity, this Solution assumes that readers have an identifiable base of repeat customers serviced by sales representatives or dealers. The Get Insights download (see Rapid Results Resources in Solution #1) provides additional options for use with retail and other types of business models where there may be thousands or even hundreds of thousands of customers. The concepts are similar; the implementation is somewhat different.

SOLUTION IN PLAIN SIGHT #1
Determine Your Who's Who of Profitability

Can you think of a *dream* customer — the one you wish you had more of? Can you think of a *nightmare* customer? You might think the difference between the dream customer and the nightmare customer means that one of them is profitable and the other is not ... even if the nightmare customer is providing lots of revenue. Management teams are often surprised by the lack of profitability of their so-called dream customers and sometimes find a nightmare customer is very profitable, or vice versa. Until you get a handle on customer profitability, you won't know which is which. But if accounting measures aren't the answer, what is?

The rapid-results approach for measuring your Profitable Customer Ratio is to ask yourself the right *qualitative* questions related to profitable and unprofitable customer behaviors that really impact your specific business, and segment them to determine who is highly profitable, marginally profitable, and unprofitable (see Figure 3). It's a little bit like looking at dream and nightmare customers in terms of instinctively knowing Who's Who, only more reflective of your unique profitability factors.

Figure 3: **THE CUSTOMER PROFITABILITY DIAMOND**

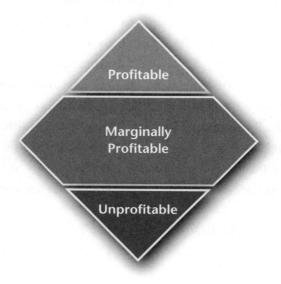

Think about it. Is there a difference in profitability between customers who negotiate aggressively, demand rush orders, pay late or have a high hassle factor and those who work closely in partnership with you? Absolutely. Are those qualitative factors observable? Absolutely.

The right selection of Who's Who qualitative factors is different for every company, and many aren't immediately obvious, but have a huge impact. When you focus on those that are most relevant for *your* specific business, you can create your initial Customer Profitability Diamond in less than an afternoon and get a "good is good enough" sense of who is highly profitable, who is marginally profitable, and who is unprofitable. Then, you can make good decisions on how to manage your customer base to improve your bottom line.

This process is very easy conceptually, but there are a few nuances to getting it right and to being able to construct your Diamond quickly and easily, especially if you have a large number of customers or a broad range of products or services. The Customer Profitability Diamond resources provide step-by-step instructions for developing your Diamond in a way that keeps the workload manageable and creates instant impact across your organization.

 Rapid Results Resources: Download the Customer Profitability Diamond and related Resources you can share with your team at www.ProfitInPlainSight.com/GetInsights and you will undoubtedly be surprised by your Who's Who versus what you may be thinking today.

Your Customer Profitability Diamond will determine how successfully you can implement every one of the profitability tactics and strategies in Part II of this book. You can still implement these strategies by-guess-and-by-golly, but the real power is in matching the right strategy to the customer's bottom-line contribution to your success.

Successfully Developing the Diamond ... Eventually

The owner of a wood products business was inspired to construct her Customer Profitability Diamond after learning the concept in a seminar. As it's conceptually very easy, she decided to tackle it on her own. She spent a couple of weeks developing an exhaustive list of profitability elements (instead of the recommended short list of key factors) and sent spreadsheets to her sales team asking them to rank-order each of their customers on each item on a 10-point scale, with the plan of developing an absolute score for each customer (instead of simply grouping them as shown in the Diamond). Unfortunately, she created a time-consuming nightmare by trying to get "perfect" information from somewhat myopic sales resources instead of good-is-good-enough information from a balanced cross-section of her team.

Despite her faithful follow up, three months later she was still trying to get sufficient data to complete the exercise. Wasting time reinventing the wheel and getting no usable results is what derails most businesses from achieving transformation. The time-tested resources engage more than just the sales team and interactively create the Diamond categories in less time than you're spending on e-mail.

When she finally tapped into the Rapid Results Resources, she got the insights she needed immediately and created a good-is-good-enough-for-good-decision-making Diamond with her team for their largest 100 customers within an afternoon.

Your Takeaway: Constructing your Customer Profitability Diamond is simple, but it's not easy when you try to reinvent the wheel. Go with the proven process for rapid results.

SOLUTION IN PLAIN SIGHT #2

Implement the Surprisingly Simple Three-Part Customer Profitability Diamond Strategies

Once you have your customers (or a representative subset) sorted based on the qualitative Customer Profitability Diamond factors you've selected, it's time to translate that knowledge into strategic approaches that generate significant profit increases rapidly and with integrity. You want to use the Customer Profitability Diamond to, not surprisingly, *Retain* your highly profitable customers, *Ramp Up* your marginally profitable customers, and *Restore* your unprofitable customers to Breakeven or Better.

Remember, you're trying to get enough insights for good decision-making, not precise data from an accounting perspective. This is about rapid results.

Figure 4: THE CUSTOMER PROFITABILITY DIAMOND TRANSLATES INTO PROFIT-DRIVING STRATEGIES

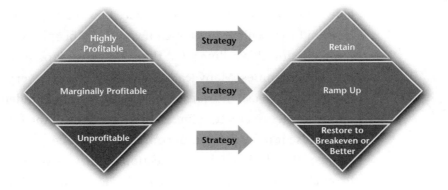

Most leaders and managers don't have an answer when polled about what their retention plans are beyond the tired old approaches of lunches, golf, and event tickets. In fact, they get a sheepish grimace on their faces. They know it's not enough, but they don't know

what else to do. Similarly, most admit that they have no specific plans for improving their marginally profitable customers or proactively dealing with unprofitable customers.

It's critical to really grasp the power of this three-pronged approach to managing customer profitability.

- What would happen if you lost one or more of the customers in your highly profitable zone? In most companies, 10 to 25 marginally profitable customers are required to replace *just one* highly profitable customer. Unless you can name those replacements right now and unless you're absolutely, positively certain that your customers in the highly profitable zone are loyal to you (ever been surprised when a customer you thought you could count on defected to the competition?), you want to develop a retention plan that goes far beyond lunches and golf games. These are the customers who are most crucial to the success of your business!

- About 5-30% of your customers in the marginally profitable zone could do more business with you at any point in time, but that will never happen if your sales people are more comfortable selling what they know than looking for new opportunities. Many leaders and sales teams never learned how to ask the questions that uncover the hidden opportunities to create value. But that's where all the fun is, because it takes you out of competing on price and changes the playing field! This section of the Customer Profitability Diamond is also an ideal place to find opportunities to reduce Unnecessary-Costs-to-Serve in creative ways, once you understand how value is perceived by your customer.

- Perceived value drives willingness-to-pay, which opens up an entirely new path to Profit — pricing for value. It is one of the fastest and easiest ways to Ramp Up the profitability of marginal customers, but many business leaders are hesitant to apply price increases. Although they all agree that they've experienced price increases from their own suppliers over the past few years, they're stuck in the mind-set that their competitive marketplace won't allow for increased prices.

- Vampire Customers in the Restore to Breakeven or Better category are costing you your dreams. The checks you could be writing for new equipment, acquisitions, or better talent are instead being written to customers who are bleeding you dry. It's not enough to know who they are. It's not enough to fire them. In five out of the six possible unprofitable customer scenarios you'll explore in Challenge #3, Ensuring Bottom-Line Growth in Profit, that's exactly the *wrong* thing to do. But you do need to deal with them immediately.

Right now, simply commit to building your Diamond and seeing who your most valuable and least valuable customers really are.

As you shift from Possibilities to Practicalities in the following section, you'll see a complete implementation road map unfold, based on this straightforward Diamond.

This is a process that pays for itself, many times over. You can stop the bleeding in less than 30 days, spot new opportunities for more profitable business within 90 days, and eliminate unnecessary costs to serve your customers within 120 days. If you are committed to results, this is where you need to start. Within a very short period of time you'll have all the tools you've been missing to proactively generate more profitable business.

The 80-20 Rule Revisited

When the lab supply company who was losing money on 33% of its customers turned the spotlight on their customers with the Customer Profitability Diamond, they transformed their business. They found that many of their blue chip accounts were, in fact, in the marginally profitable zone and that many small customers they traditionally took for granted were in their highly profitable zone.

Here's what happened next.

1. They automatically saw subtle but significant *mind-set* and *behavioral* changes throughout their organization when the Who's Who was shared broadly within the organization from the executive suite on down. They ensured that no customer was dismissed as "bad" by sharing the surprising insight that *self-inflicted wounds on the part of the company* were the largest factor in destroying the profitability of the marginally profitable and unprofitable customer segments.

2. They became more conscious of the need to take care of smaller, highly profitable customers who hadn't seemed worth their time before. The specific sales-service plans they developed went way beyond lunches and golf games and took their overall retention rate to above 90%.

3. When they stopped bending over backwards and saying "yes" without thinking to the blue chips who were not as profitable, they improved the profitability of this sector by about 12% within 3 months. They didn't say "no," they simply found ways to capture value, not only through pricing changes, but through new, billable, value-add services they developed.

4. They got seriously motivated to stop the bleeding with their Vampire Customers in the unprofitable zone and saw a 66% increase in their bottom line in the first 6 months, without having to fire more than a couple of them. They fired them gracefully and saw no negative impact.

Your Takeaway: The Customer Profitability Diamond holds the key to having everyone in your company make small, powerful, behavioral shifts that automatically improve profitability.

SOLUTION IN PLAIN SIGHT #3
Set New Goals for Your Profitable Customer Ratio

Your Customer Profitability Diamond will help you set a base line for your ratio of highly and marginally profitable customers to unprofitable customers and effectively communicate to your entire organization. Typically, you'll find something similar to this in your first Diamond.

If you have 20% of your customers in the highly profitable zone, 40% in the marginally profitable zone, and the final 40% in the unprofitable zone, your ratio is (20+40):(40) or 1.5:1 — you have 1.5 *profitable* customers for every *unprofitable* customer. Not good! When you take action on your unprofitable customers, you'll move the needle in your business in a hurry, and you'll see an immediate improvement not only in the ratio, but on your bottom line. That's something employees can grasp quickly, and will want to be part of.

This ratio will steadily improve over time as you consistently manage your customer profitability with the strategies I've outlined in this book. Customer behaviors are always changing, thus this needs to be a dynamic rebalancing process of identifying bad behaviors early and taking corrective action quickly. Over time, your sales teams will have the knowledge they need to become more selective, only doing business with those customers who mirror the characteristics of those who are highly profitable, while avoiding those who are likely to be unprofitable.

Figure 5: YOUR PROFITABLE CUSTOMER RATIO: USING THE DIAMOND TO CALCULATE A DRIVER

The 80-20 Rule Finale

The lab supply company initially had a Profitable Customer Ratio of 2:1 profitable to unprofitable customers. When they implemented the Restore to Breakeven or Better strategies they shifted that ratio to 5:1.

Imagine what that kind of shift would do for your own bottom line?

Your Takeaway: Everyone in your organization can grasp the simple concept that more is better when it comes to this ratio, far more easily than using arcane financials. It's a powerful yet overlooked communication tool to focus attention on profit-driving behaviors.

Use the Comprehensive Resources — Never Reinvent the Wheel

You've seen how powerful the Profitable Customer Ratio can be, and yet most organizations never take the time to set a base line and actively manage this very simple metric. One of the biggest problems is that all levels in the organization get caught up in measuring revenue because they simply don't have an easy way to quickly evaluate customer profitability.

Now, you do. But it only works if you use it. Your alternative is to continue to assume that higher revenues equal greater success, and yet over and over we've seen that it's not always the case.

Your path to Passion, Profit, and Growth depends on having everyone on the team taking small, subtle actions every day to proactively impact customer profitability, by serving your customers well and by being rewarded for what they do.

Some leaders are initially uncomfortable with the "good is good enough for good decision making approaches" concept. Yet based on the reactions of groups who go through the exercise of developing the Customer Profitability Diamond, it's clear that it intuitively makes sense to employees in a way that exact, yet overwhelming, spreadsheets never will. The insights that emerge and the AHA! Moments that occur when the Profitable Customer Ratio is calculated, immediately transform the level of engagement, the level of commitment to improve, and the resulting conversation on "what will it take to make it happen."

You won't achieve your transformation with business as usual or the tired approaches you may have tried in the past. Yet you don't have to reinvent the wheel. Just follow the Action Plans at the end of every chapter, and see the results you've been missing out on.

Hiccups and High Costs of Reinventing the Wheel Get Replaced by Success

You don't want to make the same mistake as the wood products CEO and many do-it-yourselfers do. Based on what she'd learned over the years about profitability, as she was waiting for her sales team to get back to her on the monster spreadsheet she'd constructed, she immediately focused on reducing costs without understanding what customers valued and what they didn't, and without really understanding that highly profitable, marginally profitable, and unprofitable customers deserve very different strategies.

She jumped the gun and cost-cut in conventional ways, including the budget for customer lunches, reduced sales representatives' expenses and travel costs, and ended up with a lot of disgruntled people on her team, customers who felt they'd been cast aside, and almost no impact on her bottom line.

She fired an unprofitable customer in a way that was highly satisfying for her, but less than graceful. Unfortunately, the customer sued for breach of contract and raised a ruckus in the industry on social media platforms that provoked a lot of tough questions from other customers. While they eventually settled out of court, a lot of damage was done, a lot of time was spent, a lot of opportunity to turn the customer around and restore them to profitability was lost. Once she worked through the Profit in Plain Sight implementation strategies, she was able to implement selective price increases that were well accepted by her customers and drove a 28% increase to her bottom line.

Instead of firing her unprofitable customers, she used the strategies to restore the majority of them to Better than Breakeven and added 16% to her bottom line. Finally, she developed a cost-effective retention plan that recognized the value of her most profitable customers.

Your Takeaway: Reinventing the wheel or reverting back to old thinking on how to drive profitability will not serve you well. You're reading this book to find solutions. Simply implement the proven solutions for more rapid results.

Summary

You've seen just how dangerous focusing only on revenue can be and you have been introduced to an easy way to determine customer profitability.

Proactively managing customer profitability the *right* way is absolutely essential, otherwise you're simply going to waste far too much time and see minimal results. You risk alienating your customers when you use tired and ineffective methods without taking the time to know Who's Who, thereby achieving *exactly* the opposite outcome to what you wanted.

You now have a straightforward framework for proactively managing customer profitability on an ongoing basis with the Customer Profitability Diamond. Retain your most profitable customers, Ramp Up your marginally profitable customers, and Restore your unprofitable customers to Breakeven or Better. While there are some very specific next steps that you'll need to take to create solid Action Plans for each of these categories of customers, simply seeing each customer in the context of the framework will start to change behaviors in your company immediately. This framework works because it provides good information for good decisions, without the complexity of accounting-based measures that fail to account for many of the intangible aspects of profitability.

You have seen how to set a base line for your Profitable Customer Ratio and how you simply need to be vigilant to improve it. Once again, it works simply by focusing attention on a problem that is too often ignored.

This isn't a nice to do for someday. You want to take action on this immediately, because you instinctively know that you have customers who are costing you money, you know you have more opportunities in your existing client base, and you know you want to get more strategic with the customers who are keeping you in business. You want to stop the leaks in your dripping profit tap, systematically and sustainably.

When you use the systematic Profit in Plain Sight Framework to improve and rebalance your profitability in safe, subtle ways, you'll start to see significant bottom-line impact in as little as 90 days.

This Works. You Can Do It. You Will Succeed.

Take these Actions

Transformation takes more than awareness and good intentions.

Assessment	**1.** Take 6 minutes to complete the "Are Your Customers Enthused?" assessment at *www.ProfitInPlainSight.com/Enthuse* to find out where your greatest opportunities lie. Forward this link to your team so that you can compare notes.
Resource	**2.** Access your Customer Profitability Diamond resources now at *www.ProfitInPlainSight.com/ GetInsights* and follow the initial instructions to delegate it for implementation.
Action Item	**3.** Schedule a team meeting to: • Ask the Tough Love questions from the beginning of this Chapter. • Review your Enthused assessment results and compare notes on where your best opportunities lie. • Review your Customer Profitability Diamond and your Profitable Customer Ratio, and then set new ratio goals.

Small Steps. Big Impact!

Five Minutes, Five Questions:
Reflect for Deeper Learning

Your first step is *internal* transformation to identify what attitudes have already shifted for you and what behaviors will follow.

1. How did the surprising statistics about customer profitability change my view of where developing a solid understanding of customer profitability should fit among our current priorities?

   _____

2. What surprises do I think will surface when we construct our Diamond?

   _____

3. How will increased visibility to our Who's Who impact behaviors within our organization? Which group(s) will experience the greatest impact?

   _____

   _____

4. What intrigues me the most about the Customer Profitability Diamond concepts? What concerns me?

   _____

   _____

5. How committed am I to find the opportunities we've been missing out on that will deliver the profitability to make the investments we want to make in our business?

   _____

Inform. Inspire. Motivate. Transform.
Enthuse. Infuse.

Leverage the Power of Whole-Brain Thinking

Unlock a Surprisingly Underutilized Opportunity for Competitive Advantage

Our creative, emotional, intuitive abilities are our greatest underutilized talent.

What would it be like to recapture the sense of exhilaration and enjoyment you felt at one time in your career?

How would your view of new opportunities shift if instead of laying problems on your desk, your employees brought creative, well-thought-out solutions?

What would it feel like to make confident decisions more quickly and easily?

Elephants are trained and domesticated as babies in India when they're tethered to a very large stake that they don't have the strength to pull up. Over time the elephant learns that its efforts are useless. As an elephant never forgets, although the stake gets proportionally smaller and smaller while the elephant grows, the elephant remains compliant, even though it could easily pull up the stake.

The elephant is stuck in the *logical* half of its brain that only knows facts from past experience. We're not so different much of the time, but fortunately we have an *emotional and intuitive* side as well that enables us to see Possibilities when our previous experiences would otherwise lead us to an erroneous conclusion.

It's time to pull up your own stake and make transformation possible. How badly do you want to break free of being tethered by the institutional memory of your firm and the "we've always done it this way" limitations of the past? You've started to untether and step into what is possible just by seeing FLY hidden in plain sight earlier, just by looking at your Profitable Customer Ratio, and just by Benchmarking your Return on People. If you're determined to change those metrics, you've joined the 1% of leaders who are truly committed to doing something different and better in order to realize their Possibilities for Passion, Profit, and Growth.

Transformation doesn't happen because you know *how* to do it. Transformation takes place when you want it badly enough to do the work and *make it happen*.

The Growth Driver Is for You When ...

... you're feeling like you've been stuck for a while with no clear road map forward;

... you've been frustrated with trying a lot of things and still not seeing the results you want; or

... your entire organization is slowing you down and keeping you from realizing your goals with "we've always done it this way" thinking.

You'll learn why and how the final Driver of Transformation — the power of right-brain, intuitive thinking — is where all the fun and passion is in your business. It's surprisingly simple to embed this kind of thinking into what you're doing every day. And if it's not a major part of your business today, you're missing out on *half* the opportunities you have to create competitive advantage that's hard to copy.

Tough Love: Ask Your Leadership Team Five Critical Questions

1. How often do we make decisions based on facts and figures in our company versus what our intuition tells us?

2. How often do we look to the past for guidance, rather than to the future for Possibilities?

3. How often do we say we embrace change on the outside, but secretly resist it on the inside?

4. When was the last time we did something truly extraordinary for our business versus business as usual?

5. How committed are we to taking action to shift from "what is" to "what is possible," by getting untethered and ready to transform challenges into opportunities?

 Rapid Results Resources: Get outside the box in ways that are beyond what we can do here, and engage your whole brain in putting the Passion, Profit, and Growth back in your business. Access "Three Uncommon Ways to Untether for Competitive Advantage." Simply follow the playful yet powerful instructions to begin your transformation. Access it now at www.ProfitInPlain Sight.com/Untether.

Now, keep untethering by exposing three myths around transformation.

Move Beyond the Myths

Which of these three myths are keeping you tethered to business as usual?

MYTH #1
Conventional Change Management Approaches Work

Let me just ask you one question: how well have they worked for you in the past?

FACT: Almost all of us find today's reality more comfortable than the thought of change, so most change efforts are doomed from the start because of the way they're perceived. We're tethered. The more effective way is to make any proposed change *something to look forward to* in the hearts and minds of your employees instead of something to be feared. Think wet diaper/dry diaper.

MYTH #2
Change Management Is Difficult and Time Consuming

There's a reason so many books have been written about change management and there's a reason why every organization still struggles with change. We make it more difficult than it is.

FACT: We're hard wired in some ways to be more comfortable with the status quo, as we see by our body's violent reactions every time our temperature goes above or below 98.6 degrees. And yet, we change every year as we grow. We change our minds, change our clothes, change where we live, and so on, at the drop of a hat. So there must be an answer to how to encourage transformational change. There is. It's called "what's in it for me" and it's about reframing anticipated *discomfort* into *comfort*.

Look at the simple logic and emotion behind the previous two Drivers. Employees instinctively know a higher Profitable Customer Ratio is better than a lower ratio, and that a higher Return on People result provides more security and opportunity than a lower one. As a result, they'll look forward to taking action to improve both of those, because of the "what's in it for me" view rather than fearing change that isn't clearly associated with benefits to them.

 MYTH #3
We Have to Keep Up

There's no question that we're being deluged with new information and management methods every day. It's not the volume that's the problem, it's the failure to filter that leads to overload.

FACT: When organizations trying to keep up get mired in "bright shiny object" syndrome, chasing multiple ideas, often not seeing them through to conclusion and rarely seeing results. For now, focus on taking action on proven fundamentals in surprising new ways. The Profit in Plain Sight Framework is flexible enough to accommodate new value-add initiatives over time. You don't just want to focus on keeping up with everybody else. Instead, you want to *leapfrog* your market. Chasing is not nearly as much fun as leading! Whether you're a man or woman, think about buying new shoes. Most often the logical brain knows the new shoes will be less comfortable physically than the well-worn pair you're replacing, but the emotional right brain knows that it's more "comfortable" to be well-turned out or in style.

Expand Your Thinking to Close the Gaps
Stay Untethered with Whole-Brain Thinking

You've already invested in many of the right things — people, technology, training, trying to stay up to speed by reading the leading business magazines and best sellers. But unless you tap into all the ingenuity and talent of whole-brain thinking, you'll miss out on opportunities and lose ground to your competitors.

Have you ever had an AHA! Moment after a good night's sleep? That's usually the sign that the creative right brain has kicked in to help out the logical left brain.

Figure 1
LEFT AND RIGHT BRAIN THINKING*

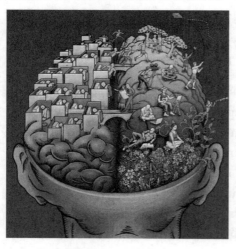

* http://wiringthebrain.blogspot.ca/2010/05/connecting-left-and-right.html

Roger Sperry won the Nobel Prize in 1981 for discovering that the brain has right and left hemispheres with distinctly different capabilities. If you're right-handed, you're likely left-brain dominant. If you're left-handed, you're likely right-brain dominant.

Since the 1990s *four* unique areas of the brain have been identified. Although we'll focus simply on activating your right brain as a starting point, what we're really moving towards is whole-brain thinking.

If you went to school in the 20th century, you will immediately recognize that your teachers hadn't been trained to teach you how to leverage both sides (and this is still far from mainstream in many schools today). Sure, you might have had an occasional art class, but you probably were taught mainly through repetition, memorization, reason, and logic, all of which are left-brain oriented. Words and spreadsheets are the tools of the left-brain thinker ... and of most businesspeople at all levels.

Right-brain learning emphasizes emotional, creative, and intuitive elements — very uncomfortable things for many businesspeople! But absolutely essential skills if you want to trigger Passion, Profit, and Growth, because that's where you can Enthuse your customers, Infuse your employees, and turn that energy into competitive advantage. We all like to think we decide based on logic, but in fact logic is merely used to support the more instinctual right-brain preferences. Furthermore, the right brain processes pictures, patterns, and concepts and helps to *simplify complexity and see solutions.*

What could you and your company achieve if everyone had more AHA! Moments when trying to overcome five stubborn market-driven challenges?

 ### GAP #1
Logical, Factual Left-Brain Thinking Rarely Provides Competitive Advantage

You and your competitors all have access to much of the same information and will draw many of the same conclusions and implement similar strategies from the pool of best practices. As a result, almost every business is increasingly seen as a commodity and that spells trouble for profitability and growth. Left-brain-dominant thinking won't help you overcome the same stubborn challenges every other leader is wrestling with. Instead, it's keeping you tethered to old patterns when dealing with:

- Market Challenges
- People Challenges

- Operational Challenges
- Financial Challenges
- Strategic Challenges

You want to untether and use your creative, intuitive talents in uncommon yet practical ways to find the Passion, Profit, and Growth that's hiding in plain sight so that you can get back to doing what you love — serving your customers in value-add ways and growing your business.

Watch and Listen

In your next meeting, observe which hand your people write with. The dominant hand is not an infallible marker of which side of their brain is dominant. Right-handed people can be right-brain dominant and vice-versa, but it can be an indicator, so just have some fun with this.

Once you know who is right-handed and who is left-handed, listen to their words. Who is predominantly using facts and figures, who is using stories, analogies, or images? Right-handed/left-brain-dominant people will use phrases like "The facts suggest …" while left-handed/right-brain-dominant people will often say "I see it this way …" or "Let's frame this a bit differently." See the difference?

Your Takeaway: Have you got a balance, or is your team skewed to the left or right brain?

GAP #2

How Often Do You Hear "Tethered" Language in Your Company When You Undertake Any Type of New Initiative?

Left-brain-dominant thinking loves to play the know-it-all, based on the facts and conclusions drawn from previous experiences. Just like the elephant, when you stay in the past rather than tapping into a creative place of Possibilities, you'll stay tethered.

How often are *you* secretly guilty of nay-saying when a subordinate comes up with a great idea or when a consultant proposes a new approach? We all are!

Listen for "tethered" language and call yourself and your people on it. If you want to put the passion back into your business, pass along the untethering download from earlier and challenge the team to see who can become the most untethered. As with workouts, you're more likely to stick with it if you have a buddy. Pair people up with a partner and trigger a conscious effort to engage in whole-brain thinking.

Your Wake-Up Call

Score your team on how often you hear this kind of language in your next meeting:

- We've always done it this way
- That wouldn't work in our industry
- We've tried that before
- It's too risky

- It would cost too much
- What if it doesn't work
- There's not enough time
- We don't have the budget

Your Takeaway: How tethered are you?

GAP #3

We Simply Don't Have Good Mechanisms for Accessing Right-Brain Thinking

It is easier and more comfortable — and dangerous — to stick with the logical, established ways we've learned over the years. The alternative seems simply too scary and uncomfortable. Yet in transformation, status quo is not an option.

Sure, there are lots of "way out there" ways to get creative in your organization, but if they're not integrated into a systematic approach, they're going to stick out like a sore thumb. And many of them deliver questionable results. It's not really about being wacko and creative; it's about tapping into intuition, judgment, imagery, and conceptual thinking to creatively reframe what we know and see it in a different way. Remember you did just this with the FLY exercise, and with the non-accounting, qualitative approach to constructing your Customer Profitability Diamond that simply gave you good-is-good-enough-for-good-decision-making insights, rather than precise but unhelpful data. You'll continue to be triggered to use whole-brain thinking throughout the rest of this book.

At this point, simply become more aware of the opportunities you're missing out on by staying tethered to left-brain thinking, because that in itself will start to create subtle shifts. The big shifts will come when you decide to be open to fully engage with the tools and resources included in this book, where left-brain and right-brain thinking are *already embedded*. You don't have to start from scratch or figure it out yourself or become an expert. Simply be open to evidence of whole-brain thinking as a Driver of Transformation and then use the straightforward, practical approaches I'm sharing with you to awaken your right brain, feed your left brain, and continue to take small steps.

Simply Weird and Wonderful, or Impactful?

Have you ever scheduled a team building session that involved a treasure hunt, daring adventures that required teams to trust and depend upon each other, or other "outside the box" approaches? If so, congratulations! That was a small step into whole-brain thinking.

The challenge is that it was probably an *event* rather than a *process* — fun and engaging, a nice break from the every day, but unfortunately quickly forgotten, and not really linked to a specific business activity.

Your Takeaway: Leveraging Whole-Brain Thinking must be a process, not an event.

Consequences
The Costly Headaches of Business as Usual

Who's got time for touchy-feely stuff like whole-brain thinking? *You* do, if you have time for e-mail every day. If you keep doing what you're doing today, you're going to stay tethered. Locked in an endless battle of the same old challenges. If that's your choice, it's OK — you're in good company with all the other business leaders who keep putting the same Challenges on the Top 10 lists each year. But is that really all there is?

All the Fun and Passion Is on the Other Side of Your Desk!

Why did you go into business?

Engineers often tell me it's because they like to build things. Service providers often say it's to solve problems. Folks in the non-profit space often identify their desire to make a difference. Business school graduates usually identify a desire to make their mark.

When I ask them how much of their day is spent actually doing those things, the silence is deafening.

Business as usual for most is sitting behind a desk, dealing with e-mail, spreadsheets, operations issues, people issues. While those are realities of business, when you're stuck in five stubborn market-driven challenges, all the fun, all the passion, and all the reasons you went into business in the first place are on the *other* side of your desk!

Your Takeaway: Put some play back in your day by listening to your customers and using your creativity to solve their problems ... at a profit.

From here on, every time you reach for some headache relief, I want you to look at that as a sign of being tethered to left-brain thinking that's not delivering the results you want — of trying to "logic-through" a challenge when in fact a more intuitive approach might lead you to a solution more quickly. Whole-brain thinking holds the key to transformation and results.

Solutions in Plain Sight
The Third Driver of Transformation Is
All in Your Head

Can you imagine what would happen to your company if you cut everyone's work week in half but still paid the same salaries?

Well, there's a good chance that your company is already in that situation because the playful exercises above have probably illustrated that you're only tapping into one-half of your employees' abilities. Your people are tethered to what they were taught — logical, left-brain thinking and it's being reinforced every day to the point where it's stifling half the talents and abilities they could be contributing.

If you don't think Whole-Brain Thinking is going to be increasingly important in your business, just look at the way social media is rising in prominence. Whether it's your cup of tea or not, Facebook, YouTube, and Pinterest are rising to the top of the search results, and all of them are based on images, not words. And while Twitter may be text-based, brevity of communicating a concept in 140 characters or less is valued much more than long-winded missives. In fact, short-burst videos are now becoming even more popular than conventional tweets. It's not about having to choose — this book is word-heavy and likely feeling very "normal" to left-brain thinkers. It's about leveraging both sides of the brain for results.

SOLUTION IN PLAIN SIGHT #1
Get Beyond Bland Words and Endless Numbers

We all know that a picture is worth a thousand words, but now that you're looking with a critical eye, you'll likely notice that rarely do we even use the full range visual and creative elements to more effectively convey our ideas, because we just don't think that way. The more left brained we are, the more words we use.

Think about the presentations you've either made yourself or sat through in the past month. Did they engage you? Excite you?

Were there strong takeaways? Or were you bored, surreptitiously checking e-mail on your smart phone under the table? Did anything stick afterwards? Think about the proposals you prepare for prospects. Are they completely logic driven with features, benefits, and prices rather than unexpected value that triggers right-brain decision making?

Think about what comes across your desk every day. Spreadsheets. Tedious reports. Long-winded e-mails that rehash old information. Mind-numbing policy and procedure binders. Strategic plans filled with facts and figures. There's too much information and too little insight.

Next time you or one of your team are preparing to present at a meeting, look at the ratio of words to images on the slides being presented or handouts being provided. Yes, there's a time for words and numbers, but a graph or graphic is often more powerful. We tend to prepare slides so that we can read from them, rather than prepare them to communicate effectively. Try to reverse the ratio to trigger whole-brain thinking. If 100% of the message is in words, try to replace them with just one powerful image on each slide. If it's 80-20, make it 20-80. Get extreme for the first little while. Surprisingly, only 25% of people think exclusively in words yet visual thinking is common in 60-65% of the population.[2] With a little practice, you and your team will get in the habit of using both sides of your brain power.

My Own Embarrassing Moment

During my teaching in the MBA and PhD programs at the University of British Columbia, I compared retention rates of material taught from word-heavy slides to those that had

---

[2] Michel Marie Deza and Elena Deza, Encyclopedia of Distances, 2nd ed. (Berlin: Springer, 2009) at p 526.

images and just a couple of words, if any. When prompted by images at the end of a 5-week course, the students readily recalled the concepts and takeaways they represented. Recall was almost non-existent for word-heavy slides.

Tapping into the power of the right brain requires vigilance. When I undertook executive-level speaking engagements, I forgot everything I'd learned. I had slides full of very impressive data and research. Lordy, did I have logic on my side. But in the early days I failed to inspire the participants to take action. Sound familiar? I'd failed to tap into the emotional right brain, which drives instinctive response, engagement, and buy-in. Instead, I'd data-dumped my audience into a comatose state, despite my good intentions.

It was a humbling experience of how easy it is to slip back into the comfort of logic and forgo the power of emotion.

Your Takeaway: Be vigilant!

 ### SOLUTION IN PLAIN SIGHT #2
Whole-Brain Thinking Delivers Deeper Insights and Better Decisions

All of us have access to both sides of the brain and we all have the opportunity to develop both sides. However, in business we most often use logic and reason to try to overcome five stubborn market-driven challenges. Sometimes we need intuition and uncommon approaches. Sometimes we need to visualize things differently.

Whole-brain thinking that encourages creative, intuitive solutions generates many more options than you can ever hope to do with just logical, rational thinking.

The diagram in Figure 2 illustrates all the different elements of whole-brain thinking and it's probably a bit overwhelming — if so, good! I'm sharing it because it's easy to talk about whole-brain thinking but hard to visualize exactly what that means. Just absorb the high points — that there are many, many ways that your employees receive and process information and many ways they can bring their creativity to create transformational breakthroughs.

Components of Whole-Brain Thinking

If you don't believe that whole-brain thinking matters, then think back to when you were a kid. Did you like to climb trees or get your hands dirty? That's Concrete Experience. Can you still sing along to songs you knew in high school? That's the Musical Element. Hmmm, did you perhaps try a few substances you shouldn't have while still underage? That's Active Experimentation! How often did you indulge in daydreams? That's an aspect of Reflection and Observation. Play sports? That's the Kinesthetic engaging. Camping? Your inner Naturalist was at work. Play with Lego? That's the Visual Spatial aspect. Hang out with friends? Intrapersonal. Crave alone time away from your parents? That's your Interpersonal self. Did you ever want to be an astronaut? Your Abstract Conceptualization kicked in there.

Math and Linguistics were about all that we got from our formal schooling — reading, writing, and arithmetic. How much richer was your childhood for all the *other* aspects of your brain that you were using and learning from? How often do you do any of those whole-brain things today? And we wonder why creativity and passion is lacking in most of our workplaces!

Many businesspeople struggle to put elements such as experimentation, reflection, social, or visual elements into practice, yet you have people in your organization (and customers) for whom that's their preferred way to learn and engage. That's where the systematic Profit in Plain Sight Framework and resources will be invaluable to you, as each and every one of them has an embedded whole-brain component to complement and enhance left-brain

Figure 2: THE MANY WAYS TO TRIGGER WHOLE-BRAIN THINKINGS

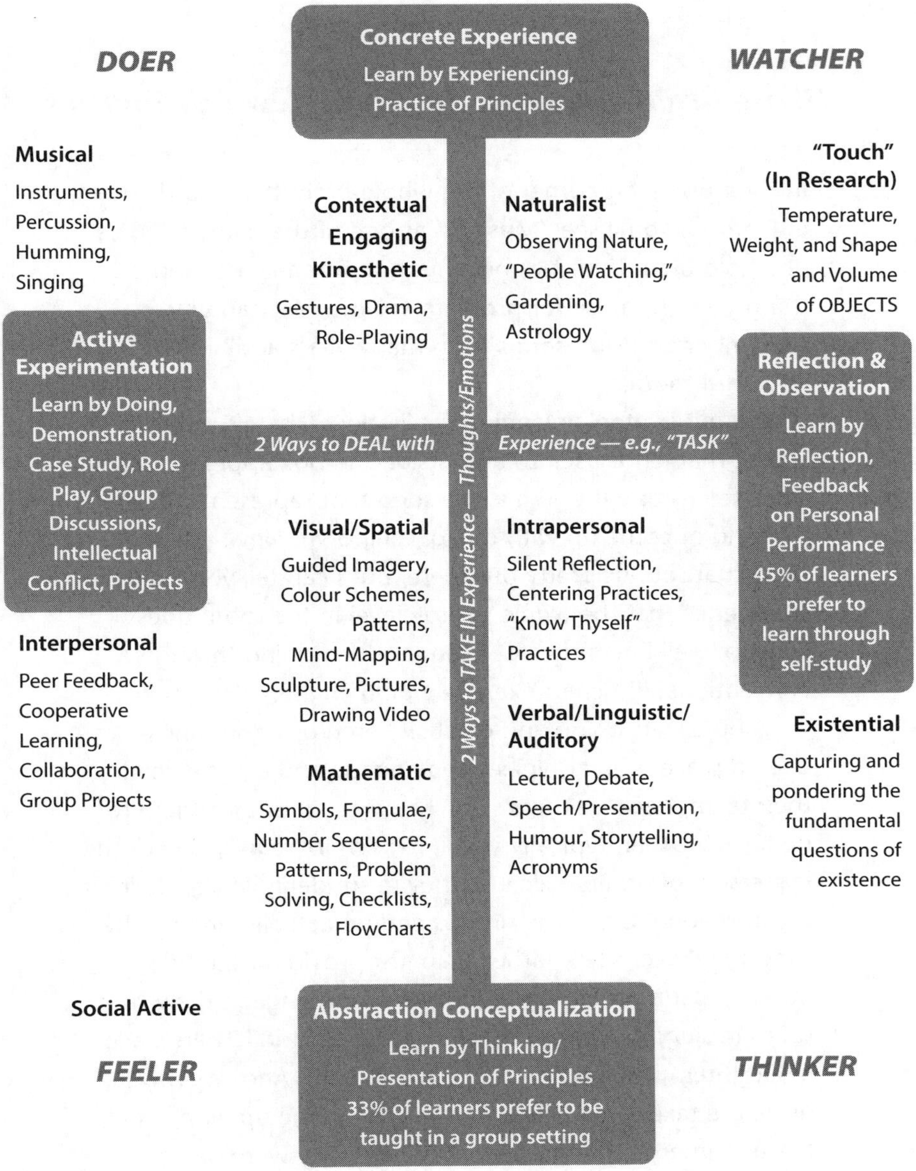

DOER

WATCHER

Concrete Experience
Learn by Experiencing,
Practice of Principles

Musical

Instruments,
Percussion,
Humming,
Singing

**Contextual
Engaging
Kinesthetic**

Gestures, Drama,
Role-Playing

Naturalist

Observing Nature,
"People Watching,"
Gardening,
Astrology

**"Touch"
(In Research)**

Temperature,
Weight, and Shape
and Volume
of OBJECTS

**Active
Experimentation**

Learn by Doing,
Demonstration,
Case Study, Role
Play, Group
Discussions,
Intellectual
Conflict, Projects

2 Ways to DEAL with

2 Ways to TAKE IN Experience — Thoughts/Emotions

Experience — e.g., "TASK"

**Reflection &
Observation**

Learn by
Reflection,
Feedback
on Personal
Performance
45% of learners
prefer to
learn through
self-study

Visual/Spatial

Guided Imagery,
Colour Schemes,
Patterns,
Mind-Mapping,
Sculpture, Pictures,
Drawing Video

Intrapersonal

Silent Reflection,
Centering Practices,
"Know Thyself"
Practices

Interpersonal

Peer Feedback,
Cooperative
Learning,
Collaboration,
Group Projects

Mathematic

Symbols, Formulae,
Number Sequences,
Patterns, Problem
Solving, Checklists,
Flowcharts

**Verbal/Linguistic/
Auditory**

Lecture, Debate,
Speech/Presentation,
Humour, Storytelling,
Acronyms

Existential

Capturing and
pondering the
fundamental
questions of
existence

Social Active

FEELER

Abstraction Conceptualization
Learn by Thinking/
Presentation of Principles
33% of learners prefer to be
taught in a group setting

THINKER

thinking. Simply follow the Action Plans to integrate this powerful tool into your organization without reinventing any wheels.

Whole-Brain Thinking Uncovers New Possibilities

In the upper, left corner of the whole-brain thinking diagram in Figure 2 you'll see "Musical" as one of the many triggers of whole-brain thinking, but music is probably not something you often use for problem solving. Yet can you remember and sing songs from many years ago? Music is a powerful trigger.

During strategic planning facilitations, there's a specific aspect that lends itself to an outside-the-box approach. I ask small teams to either think of a song that represents their thinking or come up with one of their own. Now, you may think that sounds pretty out there, but I can tell you from experience that the whole energy level in the room goes way up, well beyond what sitting around going through a conventional flip-chart exercise would create.

A buzz gets going and creativity emerges from unexpected places. Quiet types often engage and actually lead their team, because there's finally a mechanism for them to be heard. Other, typically vocal, folks more readily accept the leadership of others, because they're suddenly out of their comfort zone. Often the groups end up actually singing the song they've chosen, rather than just providing the title, others pull up a song on their iPhone and engage the whole room in singing along, because people "get it." There's a lot of laughter, which is a sign of engagement. And when we distill the takeaways from what they've come up with, clear themes emerge that go beyond where they were before.

It's not creativity for creativity's sake. It's whole-brain thinking for results.

I don't expect you to turn your next meeting into a singing, dancing extravaganza. Simply bring your awareness to the talent and skills that you're missing out on that will provide new ways to overcome your top Challenges.

Your Takeaway: Your opportunities to trigger whole-brain thinking are unlimited, when you put your mind to it!

SOLUTION IN PLAIN SIGHT #3
The Journey of a Thousand Miles Begins With a Single Step

Confucius said that a long time ago and he was right. Transformation does not happen overnight, and neither does untethering from business as usual. The most important thing is just to keep forward momentum going, and I want you to do that by taking very small steps with your team to encourage whole-brain thinking. Simply be open to the learning in five stubborn market-driven challenges that follow, by starting to develop a sense of the hidden Possibilities in your business as you use the Drivers of Transformation and work through the resources provided. I'll continue to embed small steps in everything that follows — all you have to do is keep turning the pages to untether and transform your challenges into opportunities.

A Simple Regimen Delivers Results

When I decided to check an item off my bucket list by climbing Kilimanjaro as a fundraiser for the Alzheimer Society in 2006, a lot of my friends laughed at me, because *I don't hike and I don't "do hills."* It was way outside my comfort zone, because I had no idea if I could hike uphill for 8 hours a day for a full 5 days in thin air. I was tethered by my past experiences.

Fortunately, an experienced climber laid out a training regimen based on climbing a local mountain trail known in Vancouver as Mother Nature's Stairmaster — the Grouse Grind. At about 3000 vertical feet, it's the same as climbing to the top of the old Sears Tower in Chicago (now the Willis Tower) *twice*. It's steep, it's grueling and Vancouverites of all ages use it all the time to stay in shape. That structured, doable training approach helped me step beyond thinking about whether or not I could do the entire climb and literally take small steps towards my goal. By trusting her experience, I went to a place of Possibilities, made the commitment, and put in effort that was easier than I expected. Following her system untethered me.

I transformed from a non-hiker into someone who could climb the highest free-standing mountain in the world, almost *twice* the height of Mount Baker in Washington State. I trained for it in just three weekly sessions over ten weeks, in less time per week than I was spending on e-mail. And I can say that the view at sunrise from 19,341 feet above sea level made everything in my in-box at that moment completely irrelevant.

Did you notice that I just engaged your right brain with visual images of a Stairmaster, the Willis Tower and Mount Baker instead of simply quoting the elevations?

Your Takeaway: Small steps and good guidance are all that's required to easily move beyond your tethered state.

Use the Comprehensive Resources — Never Reinvent the Wheel

As you've seen with these examples, whole-brain thinking is surprisingly easy to trigger, and remarkably impactful. You also saw how easy it is to slip back into old ways when I shared my own embarrassing story. The good news is that you don't have to reinvent any wheels to start benefiting from the power of Whole-Brain Thinking.

First, it's already embedded within this book and within all the downloadable resources. Simply use them and watch the shift happen. Second, you'll be prompted at the end of each chapter to listen for clues in your everyday interactions with others that may indicate that your organization has slipped back into logic-focused, left-brain thinking at the expense of more creative approaches. Simply bring some awareness to this possibility and then go with the flow. Before you know it, whole-brain thinking will be just as commonplace for you as left-brain thinking is today.

Skeptics Became Converts

During a strategic planning facilitation, I asked a team to tap into their whole-brain thinking to break a deadlock over strategic priorities. I asked them to put the flip chart aside and instead, to flip through a variety of magazines and find an image that best expressed what they felt needed to be their focus.

Despite some initial reluctance to fool around with such silliness versus continuing the heated discussion, tempers cooled and the energy in the room visibly increased over the next 10 minutes as they had a bit of fun tearing out pictures and posting them on the wall. One picture in particular got a huge laugh of recognition out of the group when the [female] CEO posted it. It was a picture of a filthy, worn-out engine with the slogan, "She's a little cranky and needs a good clean up." Well, that became a metaphor for what was going on in the organization as well as some challenges various members of the team were experiencing with the CEO. Fortunately, she rolled with the punches, having selected the photo herself!

As we re-sorted all the other photos, many of them had a clean-up/streamline theme, something that hadn't emerged in the verbal discussions. And it became crystal clear to the group where they needed to start.

Your Takeaway: Tired of deadlocked discussions? Step outside the norm to trigger playful emotions rather than pedantic positions on an issue.

Summary

Leveraging the power of whole-brain thinking is the key to overcoming the most stubborn challenges in your business. Unless you develop and practice it, you'll remain tethered to the ways of doing business that are keeping you stuck in an endless cycle. Relying on logical left-brain thinking costs you time as you rehash the obvious. It drives huge hidden costs into your business as you overlook opportunities to lead your market by providing value to your customers in uncommon ways.

You've found out that the ways you have been taught in the past developed very strong left-brain thinking skills but did little to develop your creative and intuitive right brain. As a result, you've been tethered to ideas based solely on logic and are missing out on the opportunities that are easily available to you to create results more quickly and easily by using whole-brain thinking.

Your Solution is in Plain Sight. As with all things in business, developing whole-brain thinking is an ongoing process. It's simple and it doesn't require any more time than what you're spending today, but it's not easy unless you are consciously aware and taking small steps to embed it across your organization.

This is not a nice to do. This is a Driver that holds the key to your transformational efforts. The same thinking that's keeping you stuck in the same five stubborn market-driven challenges as many other leaders won't break you free of it.

For now, your greatest takeaway is to know your experiences reading *Profit in Plain Sight* will support your whole-brain transformation. You may not even notice the left-brain and right-brain thinking embedded throughout the book ... but it's there. It's in fact-sharing and story-telling; it's in the different types of questions you'll ponder; and it's definitely in the very unusual strategies and tactics that I'll recommend that blend logic and intuition, hard data and creativity seamlessly. In sharing these thought processes with clients over the past dozen years, I've seen them change the way they look at their business and transform challenges into opportunities more quickly and easily than they could have imagined.

Martin Luther King and Steve Jobs were famous for their presentations and speeches that used powerful emotions and images (even in the absence of PowerPoint!) to engage right-brain thinking in seeing Possibilities and deciding to take action. Now it's accessible to you.

This Works. You Can Do It. You Will Succeed.

Take these Actions

Transformation takes more than awareness and good intentions.

Assessment	1. If you haven't yet completed the Enthuse and Infuse assessments, do them now at *www.ProfitInPlainSight.com/Enthuse* and *www.ProfitInPlainSight.com/Infuse*. Send the link to your team and ask them to take the assessments so that you can compare notes.
Resource	2. Access "Three Uncommon Ways to Untether for Competitive Advantage" at *www.ProfitInPlain Sight.com/Untether*. Follow the instructions and start your untethering process. Pass this along to your team as well or consider giving each team a copy of this book and working through it together.
Action Item	3. Schedule a team meeting to: • Ask the Tough Love questions from the beginning of this Chapter. • Hold each other accountable when you hear "tethered" language or observe left-brain-dominated thinking. • Review your Enthuse and Infuse assessment results and compare notes on the untethering process. 4. If you haven't already taken advantage of the Reflective process in previous chapters, make a personal commitment to use that valuable right-brain practice starting now. Take just five minutes to deeply ponder the questions below. You may find it useful to write your thoughts in the space provided or you may simply want to

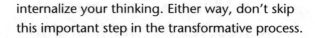 internalize your thinking. Either way, don't skip this important step in the transformative process.

Small Steps. Big Impact!

Five Minutes, Five Questions:
Reflect for Deeper Learning

Your first step is *internal* transformation, to identify what attitudes have already shifted, and what behaviors will follow.

1. What was my intuitive (gut) reaction to the tethered concept? Did it ring true for me and for our organization?

   _____

2. What emotions came up for me as I looked at the state of our business today and evaluated the Possibilities of whole-brain thinking?

   _____

3. Where will our greatest challenges lie in engaging our people to follow us on this journey and how can I lead by example to overcome them?

   _____

   _____

4. What is the *worst-case* scenario (yes, worst-case) that could happen when we embrace whole-brain thinking as a *transformative approach* for our business?

   _____

   _____

5. What is the *best-case* scenario for our business if we continue with the *status quo*?

   _____

Inform. Inspire. Motivate. Transform.
Infuse. Enthuse.

SUMMARY Start With Possibilities

In Part I, Start with Possibilities, you prepared to transform your most stubborn market challenges into Passion, Profit, and Growth. You saw how the systematic Profit in Plain Sight Framework helps speed your transformation as you overcome each of five stubborn market-driven challenges that are holding your business back. With the Three Drivers of Transformation, you learned how to spotlight Possibilities that are hidden in plain sight.

- **Your Passion Driver: Your Return on People:** You shattered your speed barriers with the Profit-per-Employee Benchmark and saw how it can ignite pride and passion within your employees. Now, challenge them to use their talents and skills to help make your firm the best in your industry.

- **Your Profit Driver: Your Profitable Customer Ratio:** You discovered an easy way to identify your Who's Who of Profitability. You'll apply the Customer Profitability Diamond to make good decisions and proactively manage your customer profitability as you implement the Solutions in Plain Sight that follow.

- **Your Growth Driver: Leverage the Power of Whole-Brain Thinking:** You received a gentle wake-up call that a combination of left-brain/logical thinking and right-brain/intuitive thinking offers powerful Possibilities that most of us never learned in school — Possibilities to engage 100% of your employees' talents and ingenuity.

Within these first pages, you've taken steps that will transform challenges into opportunities for Passion, Profit, and Growth.

Checklist of Action Items

Assessment	**1.** Take 6 minutes to complete the "Are Your Customers Enthused?" assessment at *www.ProfitIn PlainSight.com/Enthuse* to find out where your greatest opportunities lie. Forward this link to your team so that you can compare notes. **2.** Take 6 minutes to complete the "Are Your People Infused?" assessment at *www.ProfitInPlainSight. com/Infuse*, and send the link to your team so that you can compare notes.
Resource	**3.** Download the "Profit-per-Employee Benchmarking Report" at *www.ProfitInPlainSight.com/ Benchmark* to take action on the three Solutions in Plain Sight.
Resource	**4.** Access your Customer Profitability Diamond and related Resources now at *www.ProfitInPlain Sight.com/GetInsights* and follow the initial instructions to delegate it for implementation.
Resource	**5.** Access "Three Uncommon Ways to Untether for Competitive Advantage" at *www.ProfitInPlain Sight.com/Untether*. Follow the instructions and start your untethering process. Pass this along to your team as well or consider giving each team member a copy of this book and work through it together.
Action Item	**6.** Schedule a team meeting to complete any of these actions not already done: • Ask the Tough Love questions from the beginning of each Driver in Part I, Start with Possibilities.

- Review your Enthused assessment results and compare notes with your team on where your best opportunities lie.
- Compare notes from the Infuse assessment with your team.
- Develop your Customer Profitability Diamond and your Profitable Customer Ratio, and then set new ratio goals.
- Get a very clear picture of what you're putting on hold due to your current Profit-per-Employee and what that is costing your business, so that you can use the systematic Profit in Plain Sight Framework to achieve it. Shatter your speed limits by setting a goal that will really enable you to achieve your "Sky's the Limit" Bucket list for your business.
- Commit to implementing the Profit-per-Employee KPI as a catalyst to ignite pride and passion with your employees using the Profit-per-Employee Implementation Resources at *www.ProfitInPlainSight.com/ImplementROP*.
- Hold each other accountable when you hear "tethered" language or observe left-brain-dominated thinking.

7. If you haven't already taken advantage of the Reflective process in previous chapters, make a personal commitment to use that valuable right-brain practice starting now. Take just 5 minutes to deeply ponder the questions.

Now that you've got your Drivers as a foundation, let's dive into five stubborn market-driven challenges.

Unlock the Power of Profit in Plain Sight

These Principled Paths Provide Solutions to Transform Five Key Market-Driven Challenges into Passion, Profit, and Growth

We like to think that our customers rely on us.
And they like to think that we rely on them.

The systematic Profit in Plain Sight Framework provides Solutions that transform five stubborn market-driven challenges.

* Challenge #1: Earning Customer Loyalty and Retention

- Challenge #2: Generating Sustained and Steady Top-Line Growth
- Challenge #3: Ensuring Bottom-Line Growth in Profit
- Challenge #4: Developing a Corporate Reputation for Quality
- Challenge #5: Stimulating Innovation and Creativity and Enabling Entrepreneurship

How would it feel to be in true partnership with every customer, working together to benefit both of your businesses?

What could your business achieve if you had clear insights, not just into the products and services they buy, but into the solutions and experiences they crave?

How satisfying would it be to have your competitors frequently saying "we should have thought of that!"

You may be familiar with the story of a college professor who was teaching physics to his students and, by way of "untethering" them from their beliefs, performed an interesting demonstration. First he filled a beaker full of rocks and asked the students if it was full. Most said yes. Next he sprinkled pebbles in among the big rocks and asked the same question. Some still said yes. Then he sprinkled sand in among the rock mixture and by now I'm sure you know where this is going. Lastly, he poured water into the beaker and finally filled it right up to the top. He clearly demonstrated that when you put the big rocks in first, the beaker holds a lot more than when you start with sand and pebbles. (See Appendix 1 for more insight on how to use this straightforward concept as a catalyst that transforms your business in less time than you're spending on e-mail.)

It's a metaphor for business and life, of course. Most of us know this theory. Most of us don't do it.

In business, anything and everything to do with your customers are the big rocks.

Without them, we're not in business. When you focus first on the customer, everything else that needs to fit into your day will do so, just like the pebbles and sand. But when you fill your beaker with sand and pebbles first (like a couple of hours of busy work or e-mail), there's no room left for the big rocks.

The Shift to Practicalities Section Is for You When ...

... you want safe, practical, and sustainable ways to boost your bottom line with integrity;

... you want to drive passion into your business by making sure that every customer experience is a WOW that creates competitive advantage; and

... you want profitable growth — more customers buying more products and services at higher prices.

You'll start your transformational journey with a focus on customers at a *tactical* level so that you can gather the knowledge you need to build a proactive customer profitability management *strategy*.

Improved financials delivering tangible results will motivate your entire team to engage in the process of creating Passion, Profit, and Growth.

Put the Play Back in Your Day; Bucks on Your Bottom Line

When you put the big rocks in first to overcome the five stubborn market-driven challenges, you'll put some play back in your day and some bucks on your bottom line.

You know what it feels like to be coping with the grit. Mired in budgeting, staffing issues, operations concerns, unproductive meetings, endless reports, and daily crises. You find yourself scattering your efforts in a dozen different directions, trying to hold it together. You're trying to keep up, keep current, keep on top of things. And you've lost your perspective on the big rocks in the daily grit that's grinding you down.

Put the Big Rocks in First

Instead, get the heck out of the office. Don't just do a meet-and-greet, don't do a sales call. Instead, use the Value Creation Conversation technique you'll learn in this chapter to find out what's going on with your customers, and use that knowledge to discover your clear agenda for what *really* needs to be done.

Four out of five executives polled report that they rarely get out of the office to put their finger on the pulse of their customers and their markets and yet that's where all the fun is!

Armed with that information, you're ready to turbocharge your business with the practical road map and Resources that transform your five stubborn market-driven challenges.

The systematic Profit in Plain Sight Framework includes 57 Profit and Growth Accelerators that you can access throughout this book through Rapid Results Resources, brought together in the innovative ProfitU. The Accelerators will help you take action and reach your goals more quickly and easily, and with so many to leverage, you don't even have to use them all. But you'll want to, when you see the results from your early efforts. You just need to get started, one step at a time.

A Big Payoff from Simple Actions

A CEO was gung-ho to get started. The day after he attended a Profit in Plain Sight seminar, he spent 90 minutes to Benchmark his organization on the basis of Profit-per-Employee and set new goals. He instructed his administrative assistant to take 90 minutes to pull together the information required to construct their Customer Profitability Diamond.

Within 90 (working) hours after that, he'd convened a small team of sales, service, operations, and accounting folks and used the techniques in the Rapid Results Resources to construct their Customer Profitability Diamond in less than an afternoon. Within 90 hours after that, they'd determined how to Restore unprofitable customers to Breakeven or Better, with an immediate 50K impact on their bottom line. Within 90 days his leadership team had divided and conquered the task of conducting Value Creation Conversations with over 80 Retain and Ramp Up customers, just by taking 90 minutes a few times per week to get eyeball to eyeball with their most critical accounts. They uncovered over $300K of new business opportunities in the process.

They'd been very concerned about how they could take on such an important initiative, given that they were already busy running their business. Much to their surprise, all the other "stuff" that was clogging their To-Do Lists disappeared. The everyday business of running their business filled in the gaps around their 90-minute windows. They achieved significant results in less time than they were spending on e-mail.

Within 90 days, this was a changed organization but the transformation was just beginning.

They spent the next 90 days transforming the insights from their Value Creation Conversations into bottom-line impact. They acted on new opportunities that had surfaced, working alongside their sales representatives to reverse a disturbing trend of customers leaving for the competition. When they scheduled a full-day team workshop to hold a Root Cause Analysis Marathon to examine long-standing service issues and rid their organization of the five causes of Unnecessary-Costs-to-Serve, they eliminated over $100K of self-inflicted wounds.

With the low-hanging fruit harvested and the sludge out of their system, they recouped their investment by a factor of 10. They spent the next 90 days with a small team focused on Pricing for Value and refined their pricing based on the willingness-to-pay that they'd uncovered in their Value Creation Conversations. Once a week, they took 90 minutes to brainstorm their way through the price increase options in the 21 Safe, Sustainable Ways to Price for Value (outlined in the Rapid Results Resources) and found seven that they could apply immediately. They tested them on their unprofitable customers and fully implemented their new pricing strategies within 90 days. Just one of them increased their margins by 32%.

On a parallel path during that same 90-day window, another team explored what they'd learned about their customers' latent and emerging needs using the 21 Low-Risk, Low-Cost Paths to Innovation (also found in the Rapid Results Resources). They uncovered six new opportunities and developed implementation teams and timelines to take them forward ... 90 minutes, 90 hours and 90 days at a time.

Within 9 months, they had transformed their five stubborn market-driven challenges. They had increased their Customer Loyalty and Retention, driven Top-Line Growth to new heights, seen a 178% improvement to their Bottom-Line Growth, received positive feedback on their new "get it right the first time" approach to Quality, and mastered the art of value-add Innovation. And they had a plan for proactively managing customer profitability on an ongoing and sustained basis.

Your Takeaway: Transforming your business in less time than you're spending on e-mail is within your reach. You simply need to follow the Action Plans and take advantage of the Rapid Results Resources.

Ready to transform your Possibilities into profitable Practicalities?

Earning Customer Loyalty and Retention

Keep the Customers Who Keep You in Business from Cozying Up to Your Competition

The most successful companies attract customers with pull, rather than selling with push.

PRACTICAL SOLUTIONS ENTHUSE YOUR CUSTOMERS

Challenge #1
Customer Loyalty and Retention

SOLUTIONS:
7 Essential Elements for Value Creation

What would be possible if your customers helped you build your business, as part of building their own?

> **What would it be like** to be able to relax, knowing with certainty (not guessing) that the customers who are keeping you in business will keep doing business with you?
>
> **How would your customers respond** if your retention efforts went beyond lunches and golf and delivered uncommon value in ways that surprise and delight them?

Money's Mushrooms started as a small, family-owned business and grew into one of the biggest mushroom suppliers to grocery stores, restaurant wholesalers, and commercial food manufacturers. Over the years they expanded into several varieties of mushrooms, including exotics. They had a huge market share and earned numerous business awards.

One day they lost the Campbell's Soup account. Shortly thereafter they filed for bankruptcy. They learned the hard way that most companies rely on less than 15 customers for the profits that keep them in business. In their case, one lost customer was all it took.

They got an unwelcome surprise about the true state of Customer Loyalty and Retention. For years they had been a trusted supplier to Campbell's. They got good customer satisfaction scores from Campbell's. They held a dominant share of the mushroom market and thought they would always do business with Campbell's. However, as you know in your own business, things change. A trusted and loyal buyer leaves and is replaced by someone who has loyalties to another firm. A new or existing competitor has excess inventory to blow out at a cheap price or decides to grab market share by discounting aggressively. And before you know it, your loyal customer is doing business with someone else and you're scrambling to replace lost business.

Unless you have an effective way of keeping your finger on the pulse of loyalty, at some point *your* business is going to be in for a surprise. Loyalty programs are not the answer — most of them do more damage than good. Every time you see a mushroom in a supermarket or on your fork, ask yourself how long you would survive if your biggest customer went out of business or went to the competition.

Taking Steps to Lock in Customer Loyalty Is for You When ...

... there are a limited number of profitable customers in your market, so retaining those you have is critical to the success of your business;

... you've ever lost a customer unexpectedly whom you thought was loyal and committed to you; or

... you're looking for ways to stay top of mind with your customers without nagging them with the tired old "just checking in" approach between purchases.

Whether you're in a highly commoditized industry with cut-throat competition, churn, and constant pressure on margins or whether you don't think customer churn or turnover is a problem, you'll learn exactly how and why you want to implement the Retain and Ramp Up strategies — the first two of the 5 Rs for Proactively Managing Customer Profitability — that will help you to lock in loyalty. We looked briefly at Retain, Ramp Up and Restore in the context of Driver #2 and your Profitable Customer Ratio. The final two Rs are Regain and Reactivate. We'll look at all of them more closely in the Challenges that follow.

For now, you'll focus on the highly profitable Retain customers you identified in your Customer Profitability Diamond. You'll get inside their heads to really make sure they're on board with you, to deal with any lurking issues and to understand The 7 Essential

Elements for Value Creation that keep them profitable and with you for longer. You'll use the lessons you learn to drive increased profitability with other sectors in your customer base.

It just takes one misplaced assumption that a customer in the highly profitable category of your Diamond is loyal when in fact they're not or one wrong assumption about pricing and value in a cut-throat market to have a major impact on your bottom line.

Links in the Action Plan at the end of this chapter will help you implement a systematic road map for proactively managing all 5Rs of Customer Profitability. You'll challenge the conventional assumptions upon which you've based your profit projections, with the goal of finally leveraging straightforward, powerful tactics to drive bottom-line profitability and growth.

Tough Love: Ask Your Leadership Team Five Critical Questions

1. Does each member of the management team spend as much time as we should connecting with our most profitable customers to know *with certainty* what their intentions are to keep doing business with us ... or do we guess?

2. When was the last time we went beyond a meet-and-greet at the managerial or executive level to gain deep insights into our customers' attitudes, needs, wants, and intentions ... and then responded with value-add solutions?

3. Which of our customers have the most potential to help us grow our business ... and are they doing so today?

4. What steps have we taken to know who's a fan, who's indifferent, and who's doing business with us out of inertia or lack of a better alternative but has nothing good to say about us and, in fact, may be harming our reputation?

5. How much of our business comes from our top 15 customers? If one of them left tomorrow, do we have 10-25 new customers we could do business with quickly to replace that lost volume and profit?

 Rapid Results Resources: Take 11 minutes to complete the "Profit in Plain Sight Assessment" at www.ProfitInPlainSight.com/Profit to identify your best opportunities to increase Customer Loyalty and Retention.

Now, continue to get untethered by exposing the common myths that are taking too many organizations in the wrong direction when it comes to Customer Loyalty and Retention.

 ## Move Beyond the Myths

Which of these three myths about Customer Loyalty and Retention are leaving you vulnerable to the competition?

 ### MYTH #1
Loyalty Should Be a Major Goal for the Organization

FACT: Your *real* goal should be to keep only those customers whose needs you can satisfy *at a profit*, for two reasons. One, loyalty is not a suitable strategy for every company. (In your personal life, think restaurants versus dry cleaners. In one case, you probably want variety regardless of how they incent you to eat there all the time or how often you loyally recommend them to others. In the latter, if the dry cleaner is convenient and does a good job, you'll probably continue to use them out of inertia, regardless of whether you are truly loyal to them or whether there are incentives to do so.) In the business-to-consumer space, customers are notoriously fickle and trying to entice them to change that behavior can be an overly costly strategy. In the business-to-business space, risk mitigation is an important customer-focused reason not to expect complete loyalty — two or more suppliers are simply safer than just one. Having a goal to earn customer loyalty is a conceptual given. But it must be applied *strategically*. Have you fallen into the "keep-every-customer-at-all-costs" trap?

 MYTH #2
Customers Want a Relationship With the Firms With Which they Do Business

FACT: Not always. Most of us don't even have enough time to nurture relationships with family and friends, let alone suppliers. Sometimes we simply want to complete a transaction as quickly and easily as possible. If your product or service is of a low-risk transactional nature, respect that and eliminate any pseudo-relationship techniques. If your product or service helps them get the job done, you *will* be rewarded with some measure of loyalty. However, if your customer dynamic involves a true business partnership arrangement with shared risk, then of course a higher level of trusted interaction is appropriate. Be sure that the interactions are authentic and value-add, not simply noise. Think about what you may have experienced with Amazon. If you've ever purchased books on grieving or relationships, those were probably transitional in nature, and you probably don't want ongoing updates on new titles. However, if you're a regular romance reader or hobbyist, you might very well appreciate a higher level of ongoing interaction and recommendations.

MYTH #3

Loyal Customers Buy More, Are More Profitable, and Help Your Business Grow

FACT: Even loyal customers often spread "share of wallet" among several firms or know their value to your organization and therefore negotiate aggressively on price and other terms. Organizations typically invest a lot of sales and service dollars to maintain their relationship with "blue chip" customers without knowing how loyal they are. When you constructed your Customer Profitability Diamond you likely saw that in many cases, your smaller customers and casual buyers were in fact your most profitable, often with no loyalty efforts.

FACT: If your product or service provides considerable competitive advantage, forget the myth that your customers will help you grow through word of mouth. On the contrary, they'll want to make sure you're a best kept secret. Loyal customers can be worth their weight in gold, but just *never* underestimate their recognition of their own value.

Keeping customers who either cost your company more than they are worth or don't generate a reasonable rate of return is just plain bad strategy. Instead, you want to invest your retention efforts with your highly profitable and marginally profitable customers through value-add approaches that build authentic Loyalty and Retention. When you leverage your fans and take constructive steps to address inertia, you'll solidify more customer relationships and retain your customers longer.

Expand Your Thinking to Close the Gaps
The Critical Role of High-Touch Insights in a High-Tech World

It wasn't that long ago that the shopkeeper at the general store knew his or her customers by name, knew their likes and dislikes, and wouldn't hesitate to bring in special merchandise to meet specific needs and requests. They had real-life dialogue that built the relationship over time as customers freely shared their new or evolving needs. Of course, the shopkeeper was often the only game in town, which made *loyalty* a given, as measured by repeat purchases, even if the customer didn't care for the shopkeeper's company socially. Well, being the only game in town is no longer a reality for most companies. Recreating the simplicity of intent to know and understand your customers so that they'll do profitable business with you again and again is somewhat more complex in our technology-driven globalized environment. Yet, returning to the intent of that shopkeeper at the general store holds the key to retaining profitable customers and achieving authentic loyalty.

GAP #1
Indifference to Your Customer's Real Needs

Two-thirds of customers who leave do so because they sense indifference on the part of their supplier and they simply want to deal with someone who cares.

Unfortunately, most companies try to ensure Loyalty and Retention in exactly the wrong way, by *selling* when they should focus on *service* or by *servicing* when they should be *selling*. A mistake in either direction means you may be investing more than you can afford, or less than a good customer deserves. Those good intentions actually drive customers away, because with a one-size-fits-all approach to sales and service, customers quickly pick up on the fact that you haven't really taken the time to understand them. Their right brain picks up a sense of indifference, which impacts their decision making. Instead, you want to implement solutions that balance sales efforts with service value and that match your level of investment to how profitable your customers are to you. Without that plan, you'll invest more time and money than you should on *less* profitable customers, less on your *more* profitable customers and that makes no sense, does it?

Is It Loyalty or Resignation?

Do this exercise: Which of your suppliers are you genuinely loyal to and who are you resigned to doing business with, but feel no loyalty to? Which ones do you hear from just when they want the order, as opposed to which ones are always adding value to your business in small, subtle ways?

What makes the difference between the suppliers you're genuinely loyal to and those with whom you simply do business? Which camp would your customers place you in as a supplier? What can you learn from your experiences with your suppliers in the context of the way you build Loyalty and Retention with your customers?

Your Takeaway: It's time to take the time to understand if you've earned loyalty from your customers.

Customer Relationship Management (CRM) grabbed center stage in the 1990s as a "best practice," but make no mistake — *the company* never manages the relationship. The customer is always in the driver's seat because they are the ones who decide to engage or not to engage, to open their wallet or to choose an alternative. All the company can do is exactly what the shopkeeper did — provide the goods and services that the customer needs in a way that the customer finds pleasing and wants to continue to experience. At that point the shopkeeper has earned his or her right to profit from the relationship and look for new ways to serve the customer.

In Europe CRM systems have generally been used to deepen a company's knowledge of their customers in order to serve them better. However, in North America CRM is typically used to create pseudo-intimate relationships simply to reach more prospects more often with more offers, whether they are relevant or not. And customers are deeply dissatisfied, exhausted by the barrage, tuned out, and more fickle than ever as they feel more and more victimized by their vendors. Try to get off the mailing list from unwanted direct mail catalogs and you'll know what I mean.

Are CRM Efforts Just Plain Wrong for Your Business?

Depending on the type of business that you're in, there's a very good chance that one of the alternatives in Figure 1 is actually what your customers would prefer over "conventional relationship management," yet these are never taught in business schools or extolled in the business press. With a high-touch approach in a high-tech world, you simply want to match your efforts to your customers' wants.

Figure 1: THE ENTHUSED CUSTOMER MATRIX: MATCH
YOUR EFFORTS TO THEIR WANTS

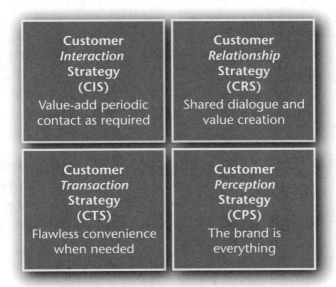

Customer
Interaction
Strategy
(CIS)
Value-add periodic
contact as required

Customer
Relationship
Strategy
(CRS)
Shared dialogue and
value creation

Customer
Transaction
Strategy
(CTS)
Flawless convenience
when needed

Customer
Perception
Strategy
(CPS)
The brand is
everything

Customer Relationship Management at Its Worst

When vendors purchased subscriber lists from a leading
industrial publication, they began a phone bombardment
with pseudo-personalized offers for other magazines and
services. I was on that list, and their offers were completely
irrelevant to my business ... yet they insisted on sending
them even after I advised them that I was a consulting
business, not a manufacturing plant!

There's nothing wrong with reaching out to see if a
potential customer has an interest in your product or service,
or in keeping in touch until the time is right for a prospect or
client to make a purchase. However, these folks throw away
money every month with unwanted marketing to someone
who will never buy forklifts and heavy machinery.

The *assumption* that I'm a qualified buyer and the subsequent bombardment is so-called Customer Relationship Management at its worst.

Your Takeaway: Appropriate value-add delivers better results than bombardment.

 Rapid Results Resources: Access "Which Strategy to Retain Customers Is Right for You?" to determine which quadrant you're in and what that means for proactively managing customer profitability at www.ProfitInPlainSight.com/Retain.

 GAP #3
The Hidden Dangers of Conventional Customer Satisfaction Measures

Most executives and managers polled say they don't do customer satisfaction surveys or only do them sporadically. They already know they're in the dark. However, if you're doing regular surveys, I have bad news for you. "Good scores" may be dangerously misleading, lulling you into a false sense of security because they *don't* correlate with either repurchase behavior or profitability. Think about it. The folks who used to supply hot meals to the airlines probably got good satisfaction surveys, until the airlines completely eliminated that service offering to cut costs. Companies that went bankrupt during a recession probably gave many of their suppliers good customer satisfaction scores. In the past few years significant tightening of the drinking and driving laws have cut liquor sales at many bars in half and yet there's nothing wrong with the service provided by the liquor wholesalers or the bars themselves. You don't have to have problems with customer satisfaction to have problems with customer retention.

Satisfaction Is Different from Loyalty

While at a conference at a very high-end resort in the southern US, I found the usual tri-fold customer survey card in my room, asking for input on absolutely every aspect of the experience — you know the one I mean. With just a short stay, I really didn't experience all the resort had to offer, thus didn't bother to fill out the form. An opportunity for them to receive feedback was lost, even though I'd formed impressions during my stay. If I had taken the time to fill it out with a lot of positives, the hotel would have said, "Great, we're doing everything right!" and hoped for a return visit. But unfortunately they'll never get any more business from me — that location is not high on my must-go-to list.

In addition to lack of response, the hotel's other problem was that their five-part scale would have required a lot of data-sifting by someone in a back room, but actually provided no useful input to management for future action and probably got lost in monthly reports produced long after the guest had left. Their well-intentioned efforts didn't capture whether I was loyal or not or whether I'd return to do more business. Does this sound familiar?

Hotels have every opportunity for meaningful interaction, but what have they done instead? They either slide the bill under the door and lose the opportunity for honest feedback at check-out that goes much beyond the meaningless "How-was-your-stay-Fine" interaction. Or worse, they've gone high-tech with a key-drop that eventually triggers sending your bill via e-mail, eliminating any opportunity for eyeball-

Consequences
The Lost Opportunities of Business as Usual

Taking action to work on Customer Loyalty and Retention might seem like a "nice to do," especially if you currently keep your customers for a long time. And who's got time for that? *You* do, if you have time for e-mail every day. You can't afford the risk of staying in the dark or the surprise of a lost critical customer. You can't afford the costs of settling for cumbersome, misleading surveys that take a lot of time to data-crunch yet deliver little meaningful information.

You *must* get the kind of transformational insights that help you truly understand how to leverage Loyalty and Retention for Profit and Growth when you're in a competitive marketplace.

Adding Value or Noise?

company-focused updates) versus information or targeted solutions that provide value to *you*? Is your firm guilty of sending marketing communications that are more focused on selling rather than genuine value-add with your customers?

Do you find yourself taking the time to respond to surveys or do you ignore them, knowing your feedback will be lost in a statistical report that lands on someone's desk months from now?

The bottom line is that the customer — not the company — always manages the relationship.

Think about the communication efforts you welcome from your suppliers versus those that you ignore. Which ones come to mind and what makes the difference? When you think of your company's relationship efforts, are they adding noise or adding value? Add yourself to your own mailing list and find out.

Your Takeaway: The first step in enthusing a customer may simply be not annoying them!

Every time you receive a survey, whether you fill it out or not, ask yourself two questions. Would I give them a high score? Am I *truly* loyal and planning to do business with them again? You're likely going to find a disconnect between the two answers. Then ask yourself how you know *with certainty* whether your customers are merely *satisfied* or truly *loyal*.

Solutions in Plain Sight
The Reason We Have Two Ears and One Mouth

How do you turn the perceived vendor indifference that drives customers away into deep insights that drive Retention and enable you and your customer to prosper together? Not with the pseudo-relationships of CRM, merciless marketing messages, customer satisfaction surveys, or data-crunching.

Gaining deep customer insights from the customers you want to Retain and with those you want to Ramp Up to drive Profit and Growth is the key (see Figure 2).

Figure 2: **TWO STRAIGHTFORWARD WAYS TO DRIVE RETENTION AND LOYALTY**

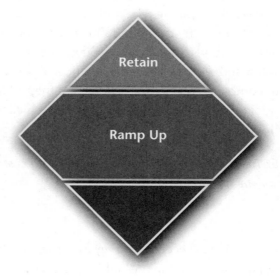

When leaders and managers at all levels answer the question on the best way to show customers they care, they usually say "talk to them." That's a great start, but *listening* to them is even more effective if you're in the Customer Relationship Strategy (CRS) quadrant of the Enthused Customer Matrix (Figure 1). Get eyeball to eyeball and simply *listen* to what two of your three critical customer categories have to say when you engage them in a meaningful dialogue (such as the Value Creation Conversations you heard about in Driver #2 and you'll learn more about shortly) instead of a meaningless meet and greet or conventional sales call. It's where all the fun is. It's where all the opportunities you're missing out on are.

It's like the shopkeeper coming out of the dark, little, back room and actually engaging at a level beyond what his or her clerks can. And it's an essential part of a successful, thriving business.

If you're in the Customer Interaction Strategy (CIS), Customer Transaction Strategy (CTS), or Customer Perception Strategy (CPS) quadrants of the matrix, the same principles apply, but with a somewhat different approach to implementation. We'll focus on the classic CRS-appropriate implementation in this book just to keep things manageable, however you can access details for the other quadrants at *www.ProfitInPlainSight.com/Retain*.

SOLUTION IN PLAIN SIGHT #1
Replace Unhelpful Customer Satisfaction Surveys With Whole-Brain, Value Creation Conversations for Deep Insights

Leaders and managers frequently wrestle with how to engage customers without the interaction being just a low-value meet-and-greet that's time-consuming but not helpful. Or they understand the importance of engaging customers at a senior level, but aren't sure how to keep it from turning into a sales call. Or they do ride-alongs with their sales reps that just feel like having an extra person on a date. None of us were ever taught the art of Value Creation Conversations, which are quite different, and much more valuable.

Just as effective sales calls require more than just a list of features and benefits, effective Value Creation Conversations require more than conventional customer satisfaction or feedback questions. To truly create value, you need to activate your customers' right brains to trigger candid, meaningful feedback that will help them realize just how much they value the relationship with you. As you saw in Driver #3, The Growth Driver, you've probably never been taught how to use whole-brain thinking for this purpose.

In the early days of the many successful business turnarounds of my career, I learned the hard way to take an executive-level approach to creating value with customers. The more I did it, the more I distilled exactly what worked well *and* what didn't. Over the past dozen years, I've worked with clients to develop Value Creation Conversation questions for each quadrant of the Enthused Customer Matrix that provoke surprisingly honest answers and result in gaining deep insights. Value Creation Conversations provide a structured yet flexible approach that creates a genuine exchange of ideas to intensify the relationship. The greatest challenges to executing the conversation well are to determine which quadrant of the Enthused Customer Matrix is applicable, as that drives the appropriate level of executive/managerial contact and the specific questions you ask. For example, you'll interact at a different level for a relationship-based scenario (CRS) versus a transaction-based scenario (CTS), and the questions will be more strategic rather than operational.

When your executive or senior leadership team connects with senior leaders in your customer's organization in a meaningful way, you'll gain insights into these 7 Essential Elements for Value Creation:

1. How much loyalty have you really earned?

2. What will it take to achieve true loyalty (and is it worth your while to do so)?

3. What are the subtle Drivers that matter most when doing business with you that you must maintain in order to keep them coming back for more, even as your business strategies change over time?

4. What are the subtle Dissatisfiers they're experiencing with you or other vendors that offer powerful opportunities for you to differentiate from your competition when you address them?

5. What opportunities for you to create and sell new products and services will reveal themselves when you use right-brain questions to tap into latent and unarticulated needs?

6. How can you safely and subtly determine how much business and how much money you're leaving on the table, take steps to close those gaps, and plant seeds to shift more decision-making in your favor?

7. Where are there overlooked opportunities to best leverage the value-add that you bring to the partnership into growth in new markets and with new customers?

As you can see, these are not areas that your sales team will ever explore in the usual course of doing business — nor should they. With all respect, they are the clerks in the shopkeeper environment, with a specific job to do and with a limited span of control and decision making. It's the shopkeeper's responsibility to seek out and act upon market insights beyond what's for sale on the shelf today. When you up-level the questions you ask and get inside the heads of the strategic decision makers in your most profitable customers (the ones you want to Retain for life), what you learn may well drive the future strategy and success of your business, as you'll see in the examples below.

Now, you may be feeling some resistance right now, because who has the time to go around shaking hands with customers with everything else already on your To-Do List? *You* do. If you have time for e-mail, you have more than enough time for Value Creation Conversations. You actually *want* to. Creatively finding solutions to customer problems is probably why you got into your business in the first place! Let's recapture that.

You may be thinking of all the reasons this would never work for your unique situation. Perhaps you have thousands or hundreds of thousands of customers all over the world. Maybe you have dealers or distributors between you and your end users. That's why there's no one-size-fits-all list of Value Creation questions that I can list here. The how to's for the nuances of the 7 Elements for Value Creation in *your* business are all available to you through the Rapid Results Resources.

Listening into the Next Century

Sam Palmisano, the former CEO of IBM, used to meet with a customer *every day* and you can bet that they weren't debating the merits of laptops versus desktop machines or how large the next order would be.

Instead, Sam was listening for the bigger needs his customers had, the needs that pointed the way to selling off the PC division to Lenovo and buying the consulting arm of PriceWaterhouseCoopers (PWC) with the proceeds. By acting on customer insights, IBM transformed into a company that didn't sell hardware, but instead sold solutions to some of the world's toughest problems, enabled by technologies of all types.

With one bold customer-inspired stroke, he reinvented a dead-ending business model from the last century into a thriving and relevant organization for the current century.

Your Takeaway: If Sam can do it, you can do it. The key lies in simply making it a way of doing business rather than an occasional event.

Simply listening to your customers drives powerful results that will transform your business ... when you do it right.

When seminar attendees see the shortcomings of conventional surveys designed to get *input* versus the concept of Value Creation Conversations designed to get *insights*, many immediately react with a "let's change our survey!" approach or consider using out-side consultants in the mistaken belief that they'll get more candor from their customers. Many want to send their sales teams out into the field to do this. Each of those approaches fails to capture the value of up-leveling in an account and engaging in meaningful dialogue. Others step up to the challenge of developing their questions, but I often see them fall into the trap of creating left-brain questions that are overly focused on *their* company, rather than right-brain questions that provoke honest and surprising responses from the *customer*. I've seen a lot of "what other products do you need" questions versus "what challenges are you still working to overcome when using our products" queries. One adds value; one does not. One organization admitted that they'd tried something similar but had forgotten to close the loop after the meeting and in doing so did more damage than good. Those are also flawed approaches. Others wrestle with "who do I see?"

 Rapid Results Resources: Find all the straight-forward answers you need when you access a systematic approach for successful Value Creation Conversations at www.ProfitInPlainSight.com/GetInsights.

Think about it in your own context. If you get yet one more survey, are you likely to take the time to really ponder your answers? If a consultant asks for an hour of your time and indicates that they're putting together a report that will go back to your supplier for review, will you participate enthusiastically with someone who really doesn't understand the business and really can't impact anything? What if you received a call from the CEO, CFO, or COO of one of your suppliers, asking if they could meet with you to better understand how they can bring more value to your business? Would you make the time and would you have a candid conversation? Leaders and managers polled unanimously say "yes!" to the last option and "no!" to all the others.

So although we'd welcome that type of interaction with our *suppliers*, we *don't* often do it with our *customers*! Nine out of ten of the leaders and managers polled say they know who their big customers are (there's that Revenue Trap again!), but rarely talk to them. Approximately 75% of them say that they leave all opportunity-spotting up to their sales representatives. They're overlooking the golden opportunity afforded by deep insights. They're stuck behind their desks. And they're missing out on all the fun in their business. Are you?

The best way to differentiate yourself from your competition is to truly show your customers that you care, not by talking but by *listening* to their needs and concerns and by *responding* in ways that save them time, save them money, solve a real problem, give them peace of mind, or make them feel good about themselves.

Pause and reread that paragraph and let it sink in. How often do you really get inside your customers' heads?

Nothing changes a corporate culture and day-to-day behavior faster than bringing the voice of the customer into the organization via a leadership team that is empowered to take action to respond.

The fastest way to inject Passion into your business is to start from the top and have every senior leader (even those not in traditionally customer-facing roles) experience the voice of the customer.

That's why Michael Dell started taking customer service hotline calls personally in the darkest days of Dell's service challenges. Do you have problems getting employees at all levels to be more customer-focused? Here's one answer to how you change your culture — it starts at the top, and if it doesn't start there, then it simply doesn't happen.

You want to get the right people involved in a deep, constructive dialogue that will actually be far more fun than just another day in the office. You want to ask the right questions in the right way, without turning this into a survey, a sales call, an interrogation, or a meet-and-greet. Access the Value Creation Conversation resources (see above) to find out how to get your leadership or management team ready and how to bring your sales team onside, how to structure this undertaking for success in each quadrant of the Enthused Customer Matrix, who to talk to, how to craft a Value Creation Conversation in a way that gets honest feedback, how to close the loop afterwards, and how to easily find the time to implement for results.

Good sales training requires more than a list of features and benefits. Developing highly effective Value Creation Conversation questions requires more than a one-size-fits-all list. Training your leadership team to use them effectively takes less time than you might think.

How Value Creation Conversations Transformed a Troubled Company

When the CEO of a high-performance sporting goods manufacturer implemented this approach, he not only transformed a marathon road trip of meet-and-greets into valuable deeper insights, but he transformed his business almost overnight. His customers told him that for the first time they felt there'd been a lot of value for *them* in the interaction and left the door open for more frequent connections. While they reaffirmed their commitment to do *some* business with him, he also found out to his dismay that he'd been losing a lot of business to his competition. They weren't buying all they could from him because he was *too difficult to do business with*.

His focus and strategy needed to change from where he was investing a lot of time in conventional salesforce productivity efforts into getting the logistics barriers out of the way so his customers would want to buy. Instead of simply trying to *push* more product into accounts that were resistant (and for good reasons), which sales productivity will never resolve, he worked hard to become the path of least resistance to *pull* customers towards him. He didn't sell a thing in those calls other than trust and credibility, but his dialogue uncovered specific essential-to-solve issues and uncovered new business opportunities worth hundreds of thousands of dollars to his firm.

Not a bad ROI for getting out of the office and having some fun in the field! What insights are awaiting you, if you simply ask? What opportunities are you missing out on if you don't ask?

Your Takeaway: Without hearing the voice of the customer, you're simply guessing what it will take to transform your business.

SOLUTION IN PLAIN SIGHT #2
React Like a Shopkeeper to Issues and Opportunities

You've listened to your largest and most profitable customers. You can cross that off the To-Do List, right? Nope. The deep insights you've gained will absolutely transform the Passion, Profit, and Growth within your company, but only if you *internalize* them, *act* on them, *close the loop* with your customers, and turn this into a *process*. But this is not another make-work project — it's play, believe me.

What would the general store shopkeeper have done with insights gained from listening to a customer? They wouldn't have nodded wisely and gone back to business as usual ... not if they wanted to stay in business. If a customer was unhappy or identified issues, the shopkeeper would make it right ... and make more sales.

If the shopkeeper found out that a local customer was going into the next town to buy items that the shopkeeper could provide, he or she would bring in the inventory and reclaim those sales. If the customer described a need that required a product the shopkeeper had never seen, the shopkeeper would probably scratch his or her head and promise to see what could be done to track it down. The next time the customer walked into the store, the shopkeeper wouldn't leave them hanging, feeling unheard. Instead, they'd receive an update or the product ... leading to more sales! All of a sudden, the relationship has deepened, the shopkeeper is really enjoying solving problems *and* is doing more business.

How to Translate Good Intentions into Profit and Growth

When well-intentioned leaders and managers make rash promises during conventional meetings with customers, they swamp themselves and their organizations by trying to act on every one of the resulting To Do's. With Value Creation Conversations you'll learn to acknowledge what you've heard without making any rash promises, and to synthesize what you've heard into a high-impact action plan. Your organization won't be overwhelmed with unnecessary work and instead will stay focused on what *really* needs to happen for transformation.

The 7 Essential Elements for Value Creation provide the insights you've been missing to resolve every single one of the five stubborn market-driven challenges. During the Conversations, you'll spot low-hanging fruit that leads to Top-Line and Bottom-Line Growth. You'll see trends, patterns, and issues that offer opportunities to differentiate from your competition via Quality. You'll uncover opportunities to capitalize on latent or emerging needs through Innovation. You'll discover the irritants that may be impacting Loyalty and Retention by driving your customers away. You'll divide and conquer the workload to keep transformation doable. All of these are proven strategies to impact Passion, Profit, and Growth as you engage your organization in making it happen.

Conducting your first round of Value Creation Conversations is going to take a time commitment. Your executive level should plan on the equivalent of 90 minutes once per week for 7-10 weeks (compress the elapsed time if your customer base lends itself to a road trip approach). Is that doable? Yes. For most executives, that will equate to only about 20% of the time they spend on e-mail. When you think about which activity delivers more value to your business, it becomes clear that finding the time to do this is essential, not optional, and only you can decide if you'll make it happen. The Resources show you the easy way to recapture time that not only enables you to hold the conversations, but go home at a decent hour without a full briefcase!

Conversations Shock CEO

One CEO in the safety equipment business who implemented the Value Creation Conversations in 90 minutes just once a week — considerably less time than he was spending on e-mail — was shocked by what he uncovered.

He found that he was *not* the preferred vendor for his largest, most profitable customers — the ones keeping him in business. In fact, he was only getting the dregs and his competitors were getting a lot more business from "his" customers! In four out of five cases, they didn't even know about a product line that he'd been coaxing and cajoling his representatives to sell for over a year. He also found where he was under-pricing and uncovered needs for new products that he could develop and provide.

Simply meeting face-to-face to deepen his business relationships yielded insights that more than *doubled* his business growth and bottom line within 6 months.

SOLUTION IN PLAIN SIGHT #3

Close the Loop Because All of the Value Is in the Follow-Through

Once you've determined which of the Enthused Customer Matrix quadrants fit most of your customers and gained deep insights from your Value Creation Conversations, you'll finally have all the information you've been missing to generate authentic customer Retention.

Put yourself back in context again. What if you took the time with one of your suppliers to outline some opportunities and irritants of doing business together? What if you honestly shared where your business is going, some of your challenges, and your hopes and dreams for the future? What if you took the time to identify real problems you need solved that would make you more successful? And what if the next time you heard from that supplier, it was a sales rep trying to sell you what he's always sold?

A Value Creation Conversation can't be a one-time event. You want to turn your initial outreach into a Value Creation feedback loop that deepens the relationship and becomes a sustainable business practice.

The shopkeeper continues the dialogue every time the customer comes into the shop, letting them know that an issue has been resolved, that a new product is on its way, that a special request is still in progress, or perhaps even that an issue or special request can't be accommodated. As long as the customer knows they've been heard and that best efforts have been made, they will feel valued.

How do you do that? There are specific recommendations in the Value Creation Conversation resources on how to close the loop (and when) and then how to keep the process evergreen, but essentially it's as easy as getting in the habit of just periodically picking up the phone and asking one or two of your questions throughout the year to keep the dialogue going.

Your salespeople can do what they do best — generate business — while you do what you do best — lead your organization into the future based on market insights. You'll touch base with your customers on an executive level in high-impact/low-effort ways to keep momentum going and you'll help your team dynamically balance the optimal time and effort invested in each customer — all in less time than you might think.

A Second Chance

A key executive of a cabinet manufacturer confessed that the first time they reached out to customers, they neglected to close the gap, and found some customer backlash as a result. It was the problem of indifference again — the customer had invested time to genuinely engage with the supplier, but the resulting silence conveyed indifference.

As a result of seeing this information in a seminar, the executive recommitted to closing the loop, and has since turned his initial outreach into an ongoing conversation and dialogue with the customers his firm most wants to retain. By making it a process and a way of doing business, he's turned it into an ongoing opportunity to develop deeper connections in very little time.

Your Takeaway: If you don't close the loop, you're effectively closing the door.

Knowledge Trumps Perception

As you take action, make sure you're responding to what you've actually *learned* from your Value Creation Conversations, not merely reflecting your previous *perceptions*. Too many companies *think* they know their customers — what they want and where improvements are needed. Even customers who may not want a relationship want to be heard, understood, and find out how to strengthen their own business by doing business with you.

The 7 Essential Elements of Value Creation help you understand the "job" your company is being "hired" to do, and naturally surface opportunities for profit and growth. When you guess, you waste a lot of time, energy, and money.

What's Really in It for You When You Turn Work into Play?

If you want to get your leadership, management, sales, and service teams seriously motivated to get on board with you, walk them through this quick back-of-the-napkin calculation, and simply make some educated guesses to identify the scale of your opportunities. For example, in each of the instances in Figure 3, ballpark whether the value to your firm is $500, $5000, $50,000, $500,000, $5 million, or $50 million, or pick a number in between that feels right. This is right-brain intuition at work, not left-brain exactness! Take just a couple of minutes right now instead of skipping past these all-important questions. You may be very surprised what surfaces.

Figure 3: THE VALUE OF A VALUE CREATION CONVERSATION?

What is it worth to us, just this year, to retain just one more Highly Profitable/Retain client that we otherwise might have lost?	$
What is it worth to us if we uncover just one new opportunity that we don't know about today with each existing Marginally Profitable/ Ramp Up client?	$
What is it worth to us to eliminate just one self-inflicted wound that's costing us money to fix that we wouldn't incur if we just got it right the first time?	$
What is it worth to us to uncover competitive information that we didn't know but will enable us to gain more market share based on how our customers perceive the value we offer?	$
What is it worth to us to uncover willingness-to-pay within our customer base that will allow us to price for value?	$
What is it worth to us to discover an unmet need that we can develop a new solution for — not just for this customer, but for the entire marketplace?	$
Total	$

Those are some big numbers. And the Solutions to transform them from a scribble on a piece of paper to tangible results on your top line and your bottom line are in Plain Sight.

Use the Comprehensive Resources — Never Reinvent the Wheel

Every leader at every level knows there's tremendous value in getting close to their customers. Initially, almost everyone wrestles with making the time to do it in a meaningful way, wrestles with the fear of what they might find out when they do, and dreads the workload that may result.

Universally, they find their fears unfounded, and that their lives actually get easier when they shift their efforts from daily tactical activities to high-impact Value Creation Conversations with customers, tailored to the relevant quadrant of their Enthused Customer Matrix. You'll learn more about the tremendous impact on their business in the numerous case studies throughout the pages that follow.

Summary

Keeping the customers who keep you in business has everything to do with understanding what level of relationship is important and then responding to the voice of the customer in ways that deliver value. Lost customers cost you not just volume, revenue, and profit, but credibility. Unhappy customers add Unnecessary-Costs-to-Serve into your business. Missed opportunities to fill latent needs don't just cost you revenue, profit, and market share today, they may just hold the key to the future of your business, but you'll never know that unless you join the many leaders at all levels who take the time to listen and see the bigger picture.

Want to stand out from the crowd? Simply surprise and enthuse your customers by connecting with them in ways that let them tell you more about their business and what your role could and should be to add value. They're stuck in the everyday minutiae, just as you are, and will welcome the opportunity to trade thoughts with you. Take 90 minutes just once a week for the next quarter, and meet with your customers.

This isn't a "nice to do" for "someday." You want to take action on this immediately, even if customer retention is not a big problem for you, because of all the other benefits that will deliver bottom line impact immediately. The insights you'll get will drive every other market strategy without the wasted time and effort that's bogging you down today.

As with all things in business, developing the relationships to secure Customer Loyalty and Retention is an ongoing process. It's easy to let it lapse and lose all the momentum you've gained. Having the right systems and tools will make it easy to transform the Challenge of Customer Loyalty and Retention into a core value-driver in your business.

You've learned how engaging your senior team with fresh ears and insightful questions serves three purposes.

1. It vividly demonstrates to your most valuable customers that you are *not* indifferent, but deeply interested, which starts to engage them and differentiate you from your competitors to improve your Retention.

2. Those deep insights provide the foundation for a comprehensive customer engagement and Retention plan, which transforms good intentions into take-it-to-the-bank impact.

3. Your wealth of insights will drive every other strategy you create to deliver profitable value to existing and new customers.

Every time you see any kind of customer survey, keep asking yourself the question: Are our customers truly loyal to us?

This Works. You Can Do It. You Will Succeed.

Take these Actions

Transformation takes more than awareness and good intentions.

Assessment	1. Take 11 minutes to complete the "Profit in Plain Sight Assessment" at *www.ProfitInPlainSight. com/Profit* and pass the link along to your team so that you can compare notes.
Resource	2. Commit to begin the process with the Value Creation Conversation Resources at *www.ProfitInPlainSight.com/GetInsights*.
Resource	3. Explore how you can make the right choices between CRS, CIS, CTS and CPS at *www.ProfitInPlainSight.com/Retain*.
Action Item	4. Schedule a team meeting to: • Ask the Tough Love questions from the beginning of this Chapter. • Hold each other accountable when you hear "tethered" language or observe left-brain-dominated thinking about your customers. • Decide how to divide and conquer the workload and complete your Value Creation Conversations. As a recommendation, have your CEO/Owner conduct Value Creation Conversations just with the customers in the Retain zone at the top of your Customer Profitability Diamond. Have second-in-command resources and other executives divide and conquer the workload to connect with your Ramp Up customers in the middle of the Diamond.

- Review your "Profit in Plain Sight Assessment" results and compare notes on where your best opportunities for Passion, Profit, and Growth exist.

Small Steps. Big Impact!

Five Minutes, Five Questions: Reflect for Deeper Learning

Your first step is *internal* transformation, to identify what attitudes have already shifted and what behaviors will follow.

1. How has my thinking changed about the types of relationships I want us to have with our customers?

   _____

2. What Possibilities exist by replacing our existing customer satisfaction tools with the Value Creation Conversation approach?

   _____

   _____

3. How effectively are we getting inside our customers' heads today and how would deep insights take our business to a new level?

   _____

   _____

4. What are the drawbacks that I anticipate in getting away from my desk and engaging our customers? What are the greatest benefits?

   _____

   _____

5. How truly committed am I to transforming the voices of our customers into bottom-line results on an effective and sustainable basis?

   _____

Inform. Inspire. Motivate. Transform.
Infuse. Enthuse.

Generating Sustained and Steady Top-Line Growth

How to Sell More Products and Services to More Customers at Higher Prices

Our best source of new business is old customers.

PRACTICAL SOLUTIONS ENTHUSE YOUR CUSTOMERS

Challenge #2
Top-Line
Growth

SOLUTIONS:
21 Safe, Sustainable
Ways to Price
for Value

How would it feel to know the secret of putting 10-50% or more on your Top Line, almost overnight?

How would strong Top-Line Growth create motivation, energy, enthusiasm, and passion among your employees?

What would sustained and steady Top-Line Growth make possible in your business?

Have you ever bought pre-washed lettuce in a bag? Did you know that it costs four to five times as much as a head of lettuce? Do you buy it gladly because it fulfills a need that you have, even though it's so much more expensive?

It looks like some of the lettuce folks figured out how to generate some significant, sustained, and steady Top-Line Growth, doesn't it? They now sell more lettuce, to more customers, at higher prices.

Why has bagged lettuce been so successful? It saves *time* versus preparing it yourself. It saves *money* versus having to buy full heads of all the different types of lettuce that you can get in one bag. It *solves a problem*, because bagged salad keeps longer than regular lettuce in the fridge, due to the value-add packaging. It provides *peace of mind* if you're boating or camping where clean water for rinsing is scarce. And it's a *feel-good* — now anybody can serve an exotic restaurant-style salad in mere minutes.

The lettuce folks hit a home run with something as simple and basic as lettuce. Surely your business with all of its complexities and multitude of products and services has the same opportunities to generate Top-Line Growth ... if you know where to look.

Get ready to "find the lettuce" in *your* business so that you can price for value.

Top-Line Growth Solutions Are for You When ...

... you want to generate growth by selling *new products* to *existing* customers;

... you want to grow by selling *existing* and *new* products to *existing* and *new* customers, at higher profits; and

... you want to expand to *new markets* in ways that are efficient and cost-effective.

The nirvana of growth — more product and service sales, to more customers, at higher prices — is within your reach.

Tough Love: Ask Your Leadership Team Five Critical Questions

1. What products and services do we already have that simply aren't being sold effectively?

2. How well do we understand the "job" that our products and services are being "hired" to do?

3. How often are we looking beyond our product set to provide complete solutions?

4. What lettuce-type pricing opportunities are we overlooking because we don't fully understand willingness-to-pay in various customer segments?

5. How effectively do we optimize our business from every customer we've *ever* done business with, not just those that are active today?

 Rapid Results Resources: Want to know exactly how to find your lettuce? Access Resources at www.ProfitInPlainSight.com/FindYourLettuce.

Now, keep untethering as we expose some murky myths surrounding growth.

Move Beyond the Myths

Which of these three myths needlessly complicate your Top-Line Growth efforts?

MYTH #1
New Customers Are the Best Way to Grow

FACT: Every business needs new customers to grow and survive, because the wants and needs of existing customers will change, their preferences in suppliers will change, and some will go out of business. Unfortunately, companies too often chase Top-Line Growth from new customers to the *detriment* of optimizing their current business. Instead of winning back lost customers and finding ways to price for value with existing customers, salespeople tend to focus simply on new revenue, rather than overall profit, often because that's what they're incented to do. They increasingly sell to marginal customers and market spaces that cost the company more than they're worth, stunting healthy profitable growth. Where are *your* sales resources and marketing dollars focused? Are you chasing new accounts or optimizing the business opportunities you have with existing and past clients?

MYTH #2
All Top-Line Growth Is Good

FACT: Have you ever increased your Top Line only to find that your profits went *down*? That's the case with approximately 40% of companies who increase their revenues in any given year! Revenue is only good if it covers the direct and indirect costs of providing your goods and services while leaving something for your bottom line. Otherwise, it's the Revenue Trap all over again. If you measure and/or compensate your sales team on revenue (or even gross margin), they will think they're doing the right thing when they bring you revenue, even if it's at any cost, just as you saw in the earlier tale of Digital Equipment's downfall. Adding more marginal or money-losing customers achieves Top-Line Growth, but destroys value in your business.

MYTH #3
New Products Are the Best Way to Grow

FACT: Every business needs new products or services, however with a 70% or greater failure rate for new products and a 90% failure rate for new startups, a lot of time is wasted chasing growth that will never materialize. That's the hard way to grow. Your Value Creation Conversations will uncover the easy way to grow by *repurposing* your existing products and services to add value in different ways just like plain, basic lettuce was repurposed, instead of spending a bundle on R&D. When it's time to explore innovation and new products for your business later in the book, two innovation frameworks will provide low-risk opportunities for success.

Expand Your Thinking to Close the Gaps
"Find your Lettuce" to Create Top-Line Growth

Conceptually, generating sustained and steady Top-Line Growth organically is simple.

Sell more products and services ...
to more customers ... at higher prices.

Too many business leaders polled are trying to accomplish growth in exactly the wrong way — by chasing new markets or acquiring new businesses. The lettuce folks didn't try to invent a new vegetable or sell to markets who had never seen lettuce before. They just repurposed their existing product to provide a *solution* instead of just a *product*. They understood the "job" their product was being "hired" to do!

Almost every business has value-add "lettuce" opportunities that will deliver sustained and steady Top-Line Growth much more quickly and easily and that will then provide the funding to chase more exotic growth strategies down the road.

If you're lacking inspiration (although you won't be after conducting your Value Creation Conversations — many opportunities will surface during those discussions), just look at the proliferation of apps for smart phones. There's an entirely new industry for products and services that save all of us time, save us money, solve a real problem, offer peace of mind, or provide a feel-good that didn't even exist a few years ago. They found the lettuce in cell phones! Apps build Customer Loyalty and Retention (Challenge #1) for the smart-phone manufacturers and generate Top-Line Growth (Challenge #2) for wireless companies due to more revenues from data usage. Although many are free, many apps create revenue for their creators. Look at how quickly many of those apps have become indispensable — I'm sure there are several that you use all the time.

A smart phone is no longer just a phone. It's an *integrated system* for managing our lives, just like this book is no longer just a book — it's an *integrated system* for managing your Profit and Growth.

 ## GAP #1
Most Sales Teams Are Overlooking the Low-Hanging Fruit

Most businesses have a 60-70% chance of selling to existing customers, a 20-40% chance of winning back a lost customer, and only a *5-20% chance* of securing a new customer. Does that feel about right in your business, when you think about it? Where do your sales representatives spend most of their time? Probably trying to close new customers, because most sales representatives love the thrill of the kill. They are hunters, not harvesters. You want to make sure you harvest all the bounty of the hard work you've invested in already in addition to chasing new customers.

Take a close look at the business you're incenting. If your sales team sees new customers as the hallmark of success, then you are overlooking rapid, easy, and less costly paths to Top-Line Growth.

It's Guts, Not Glory

A company selling packaged software solutions in a niche service industry found that mergers and acquisitions among their customers were resulting in consolidation and the belief by many customers that they had the critical mass to create an in-house software solution of their own. As a result, customers were cancelling their contracts weekly, yet the company failed to develop any type of retention strategy.

One enterprising account manager spotted a gap in the approach many of those developing their in-house solutions were using that his company could fill — they might not be able to keep the existing software contracts, but they could still retain the customer by finding new solutions that filled a new need.

He also stayed in touch with his "lost" customers to track the results they were getting with their in-house efforts. Over time, he often was able to illustrate to his accounts that they weren't driving as much revenue with their own efforts as they had by using the 3rd party software. When faced with the facts, customers gladly came back to his solution.

There wasn't a lot of glory in simply doing the right things to Retain and Regain customers ... but he remained one of the few account managers whose sales continued to be strong in an industry that was losing ground to unexpected shifts in buyer behavior.

Your Takeaway: If you're primarily recognizing and incenting new business, you're overlooking the fastest and most effective way to impact Top- and Bottom-Line Growth.

GAP #2

Many of Your Customers Can Do More Business With You

In most companies, about 5-30% of existing customers could do more business if their needs were properly identified or a better value proposition provided. What do most of your sales representatives feel most comfortable with? Probably selling what they've always sold, rather than looking for new needs or eagerly pitching new product lines.

Most of us may not even be aware that our customers could be doing more business with us, because we don't have any insights into the business they're taking to competitors that we could easily provide instead. Often we haven't done a good job educating them on new product lines or services, so they buy what they always have from us and as new needs surface, they look for new suppliers.

Are They Dead or Just Sleeping?

Eight out of ten leaders initially say they have no inactive customers, yet when we dig a little deeper, over half of them admit that their metric for measuring this is whether or not they mail a monthly statement. Most look a little shamefaced when asked if those statements actually reflect billings, or are simply automatically sent, even with a zero balance.

Mailing a monthly statement, catalog, or other form of customer contact does *not* mean you have an active customer! There are effective ways to Reactivate inactive customers to drive Top-Line Growth, but most often inactive customers simply remain below your revenue radar, although you incur costs to stay in touch. Many could do more business with you.

Your Takeaway: If you haven't heard from them for a while, it's time they heard from you.

GAP #3
Lost Business Holds More Potential than You May Think

While some companies have comprehensive lost-business processes, most of us hate to follow up with customers we've lost, because the standard easy excuse for a customer who doesn't want to hurt your feelings is to tell you that they got a better price. Well, that may be the case in some instances, but in 7 out of 10 cases there's a hidden reason you lost the business. And until you address it, you're going to lose more business. Bringing back a lost customer is your second-greatest opportunity for generating Top-Line Growth. But we all tend to avoid it.

You may not even know you've lost business in an account, if they're still buying what they always have, but are quietly taking new business to your competitors that should be coming to you. Often a customer doesn't know that you carry the product or service they need. Often a competitor was simply more proactive in finding out their needs. Often, we just don't take the time to fully understand the "job" the customer is "hiring" our product or service to do.

Leaks Are More Common than You Think

Think about your own personal habits. Do you ever stop at a convenience store for a last-minute grocery item, rather than buying it during your usual weekly shop at your favorite grocery store?

Of course you do! Your favorite store cashier still thinks they have a happy, loyal customer when they see you each week, even though corporately the store knows that you have other options, and that in their case it doesn't make sense to try to keep all of your business.

> However, in your own business, who's the "convenience store" in your industry? Where is business leaking out around the edges? It may be someone completely below your radar, but it's taking a bite out of your bottom line.
>
> *Your Takeaway: You won't know until you ask.*

Consequences
The Expensive Implications of Business as Usual

Bringing in a big new account is a lot sexier than quietly working to add value to your existing accounts, which might seem like just a "nice to do someday" — and who's got time for that? *You* do, if you have time for e-mail every day.

Every market has a limited number of highly profitable customers and every time one of your customers gives new business to a competitor, you're leaving money on the table. Top-Line Growth that could have automatically come to you, instead went to somebody else. Lost opportunity goes well beyond the immediate impact on your Top Line and erodes your position within that account, giving your competition toeholds that they may exploit until one day you find you've lost all the business in the account.

You can't afford to count on only new customers to make your numbers this year, not with all the Top-Line opportunities that are hidden in plain sight. What you want is a systematic approach to capitalize on them that's not just another make-work project, but an energizing force in your firm.

Small Shifts, Big Difference

Let's go back to the safety equipment company who discovered that they were getting the dregs while their competitors got most of the business.

In general, the salespeople were making a very comfortable living selling what they'd always sold. They felt no urgency to try to sell new products into their comfortably established accounts.

When the CEO conducted Value Creation Conversations, he realized that he had a bigger problem than just too much inventory of new product that was sitting unsold on the shelves. He needed to make changes to how customers learned about new products and he needed to incent his reps to focus on identifying new needs, not just taking orders. He needed to find ways to add value that would not only drive new business, but support value-add pricing. With that insight, the CEO was able to make small shifts in his business that made a big difference in his top line and in his bottom line.

Business as usual would never have generated those insights.

Your Takeaway: What insights are waiting for you ... if you simply ask?

Whenever you see lettuce in your local grocery store and whenever you have lettuce on your fork, ask yourself if you've taken the time and effort to "find the lettuce" in your business. We're not talking about the cheap, undifferentiated head of lettuce that almost everyone else is selling, but your special value-add mix that saves time, saves money, solves a real problem, offers peace of mind, or provides a feel-good ... and sells for five times as much.

Solutions in Plain Sight
Three Accelerators Hold the Key to
Top-Line Growth

Want to put some of the Passion back in your business? Let's employ an oh-so-simple formula for Growth and actually make it happen with specific strategies from the systematic Profit in Plain Sight Framework. It's where all the fun is!

1. **You'll sell more products and services ...** when you Ramp Up the marginally profitable customers you identified in your Customer Profitability Diamond and also use what you learned to Reactivate dormant accounts. Over time, you'll take this approach with all of your customers to drive sustainable Top-Line Growth.

2. **You'll sell to more customers ...** when you develop a strategy to Regain your lost customers, who have the second-highest potential to do business with you and when you use what you learn to *improve close rates* with new prospects for additional Top-Line impact.

3. **You'll realize higher prices ...** as your Value Creation Conversations uncover willingness-to-pay and pave the way to optimize pricing even in the most commoditized industries.

The Solutions in Plain Sight that follow will show you how to create Top-Line Growth and Bottom-Line impact within your current customer list using three of the 5Rs for Proactively Managing Customer Profitability: *Ramp Up, Regain,* and *Reactivate.* (You'll find Reactivate Strategies when you access the Rapid Results Resources referenced within this Chapter.) Just as Dorothy said in the *Wizard of Oz,* "There's no place like home" — "home" is your existing and past customers, not the ones somewhere over the rainbow. Just the fact that you're engaging and dialoguing with your customers with the Value Creation Conversations will uncover additional business and therefore Top-Line Growth.

Your goal is to look for pricing and product/service opportunities that you're not capitalizing on today. Many teams who implement the Value Creation Conversations are shocked to learn that larger checks are being written to their competition. You'll also want to listen for latent or emerging needs that will drive your *entire* growth strategy forward — with every existing customer, with new customer segments, and in new markets.

 SOLUTION IN PLAIN SIGHT #1
Sell More Products and Services With the Ramp Up Strategy

The Ramp Up Strategy creates opportunities to sell more products and services at higher prices with a value-add approach to generate Top-Line Growth, even though you'll never be "selling." Once again, you'll use your Value Creation Conversations as the catalyst for the Ramp Up Strategy, but with a slightly different focus. With Highly Profitable customers you want to Retain, you're looking primarily for loyalty and issues that need to be resolved. With Ramp Up customers, you want to Retain them too, but you're more actively looking for new opportunities to increase the amount of profitable business they could be doing with you, and understanding their willingness-to-pay for value.

When you ask the right-brain questions to spot patterns of unmet needs, you can act on the opportunities that surface during your Value Creation Conversations to save your customers time, save them money, solve a real problem, provide peace of mind, or create a feel-good. There are some nuances to looking for those needs, but they will surface when you take an *insightful* approach at the executive level rather than a *sales* approach. Getting creative with what you hear from your Ramp Up customers is one of the most enjoyable parts of your business — and probably why you went into business in the first place! When you get out from behind your desk and make it happen, you and your people will rediscover the passion that's been missing in busy-ness as usual.

If you recall the typical distribution of customer categories from the Customer Profitability Diamond in Part I (see Driver #2, Figure 5), you'll realize that there are typically a greater number of customers in the Marginally Profitable/Ramp Up zone that need to be contacted. The challenges experienced by leaders and managers who immediately grasp the benefits of this approach include some or all of the pitfalls noted below.

- Leaving it up to the owner or CEO to tackle the workload, because the rest of the team doesn't see themselves in a customer-facing role or are unclear that this is their best opportunity to gain insights that will drive the future of the company.

- Asking conventional left-brain, survey-type questions that fail to generate the candid answers that uncommon, right-brain Value Creation Conversation questions excel at revealing.

- Pouncing on clients as soon as they hear a latent need, and turning the conversation into a sales call instead of staying strategic and focused on value-add discussions.

- Wasting time trying to contact the wrong level in the company by not fully understanding the implications of the Enthused Customer Matrix (see Challenge #1, Figure 1), or asking inappropriate questions for the quadrant their clients are in.

- Failing to have a plan to effectively close the loop with each customer.

You've invested in conventional sales training for good reason. Likewise, now you want to invest the time and effort learning how to implement your Value Creation Conversations with your Ramp Up customers the *right* way to ensure you get the results you want, instead of trying to shortchange this high-potential group. The straightforward, proven ways to avoid these potential pitfalls already exist.

This aspect of the Ramp Up Strategy is not only a lot of fun, but it generates significant Top-Line Growth. Once you've seen or heard what customers are wrestling with or frustrated by in their businesses, you can engage in providing value-add *solutions* that are priced for value received, not just products and services.

How Finding the Lettuce in a Commoditized Product Delivered Top-Line Growth

When a ball bearing company implemented the Ramp Up Strategy, they found out how to sell more products and services to more customers at higher prices.

Their Value Creation Conversations helped them spot a hidden opportunity in the way that their bearings were being used to repair shop floor equipment. Many other small items were required for the repair, all stored in different places. When they created an entire repair kit with everything required, they become the preferred one-stop shop.

They saved their customers the time required to find and assemble all the repair components; saved them the time and cost of managing many small inventory items; solved the real problem of getting the repair done more quickly; and provided peace of mind that everything required would always be on hand. And, they changed the playing field on their competition by taking bearings out of the commodity space when they took their repair kit to the broader marketplace. They also earned a premium price because of the extra value they added.

They "found the lettuce" for Top-Line Growth despite having a highly commoditized product.

Your Takeaway: If differentiating from the competition is a challenge for you, find your lettuce.

 Rapid Results Resources: "Lettuce" is one of the seven straightforward Ramp Up Strategies that will transform your Top-Line Growth. While I don't have the scope in this book to do justice to them all, you can access all the details plus the Reactivate Strategy at www.ProfitInPlainSight.com/GetProactive.

 SOLUTION IN PLAIN SIGHT #2
Sell to More Customers With the Overlooked Regain Strategy

Some companies are great at conducting lost business reviews on *major* opportunities or tenders to find out why the business was lost. Most never do much with the information they get.

Most of us *avoid* talking to a customer that we know we've lost, because we're afraid of getting blasted or we're simply exhausted of hearing a price objection that we have no answer for. We dread it as much as a trip to the dentist, even though we know it's the right thing to do. Often we settle for *price* as the reason; usually it's more related to *value*. That's the same as getting a quick cleaning at the dentist when you really need a filling to stop the pain. Once again, the Value Creation Conversations hold the key to transforming pain into gain.

You won't get a candid answer by asking, "Why did we lose the business?" You really want to use the right questions to uncover why they found that another solution offered more value. If you don't find out the real reason why every single one of these customers left and invite them back, you're missing out on the significant opportunity to do business again with *20-40%* of the customers who have left or taken some of their business elsewhere.

Capitalizing on a hidden opportunity to recover lost business that you may not even know about can be even more valuable. What happens when a customer simply takes *some* of their new or existing business to other suppliers and we don't even know about it, as illustrated in the convenience store example? Most of us are *not* very good at following up on *smaller* deals or customers with whom we used to do more business, especially without the trigger of a lost bid to give us a heads-up. We may still send invoices and statements without even realizing that there's a significant lost opportunity to sell more. This strategy works for lost customers *and* for invisible lost opportunities. It delivers results you can take to the bank.

Your Value Creation Conversations ask the right questions of lost customers; the Regain Strategies show you how to turn their answers into an opportunity to invite them to do more business with you and take what you learn to drive Top-Line Growth across your *entire* customer base … at value-add prices. Lost customers are a gold mine when you take the right approach. Here's how it works.

Understanding Desired Value Creates an Entire Salad of Opportunities

A membership-based organization was facing a revolving door of customers — for every new customer they brought in, one would leave. They were planning to offer significant price reductions that they hoped would help, but fortunately decided to find out why they were *really* losing members before doing so.

They found that many of those who were leaving *enjoyed* being members and that price was *not* the real problem. *Justifying the value* to those above them who had to sign off on the (significant) membership fee was the major issue.

The organization addressed the value gap by collecting testimonials from long-time members that reflected the *bottom-line benefits* to their business that came about directly as a result of their membership. In other words, they showed how membership was not just an expense, but a tangible contributor to the success of the members' businesses. They proved that membership saved them time, made or saved them money, and helped them solve real problems. While the organization had been selling advocacy and networking for which the price was hard to justify, the members identified an *entirely different* range of other value that they received from their membership that was easy to build a business case for. When the organization sent the testimonials to the lost members along with an invoice (undiscounted) and an invitation to return, almost *50%* of the lost members came back right away, driving a significant spike in Top-Line revenue and flowing profits right to the bottom line.

When they included those same testimonials with their renewal invoice, sent to existing members, the revolving door stopped. Retention went from 50-50 to *96%*.

When they embedded the testimonials in the sales process, a one-in-one-hundred close rate skyrocketed to *one in three*.

This illustrates a classic Regain Strategy. They took it to the next level to generate Ramp Up impact when they extended what they'd learned to create more value with all of their existing customers. Once they understood the value that members were willing to pay for, they turned what they'd learned into *over a dozen* new programs and services that created new revenue streams and delivered Top-Line Growth. Instead of simply chasing new customers and losing half of them within the year, they got proactive about managing their Customer Profitability Diamond and transformed from a floundering one-trick pony selling memberships to a thriving enterprise selling value-add solutions at a profit.

They found their lettuce and sold more products and services, to more customers, at higher prices.

If this organization hadn't taken the time to find out the *real* reason they were losing members, they would have proceeded with slashing prices, which would not have solved the problem but which would have destroyed their top line *and* their bottom line.

Your Takeaway: Lost customers will come back when you address what drove them away.

 Rapid Results Resources: If this struck a chord with you because you've got lost customers but up until now you haven't had an effective approach to win them back, you'll be delighted to know that the details of the Regain Strategy used above are included in your Customer Profitability Management Resources at www. ProfitInPlainSight.com/GetProactive.

While testimonials are simply one tactic and may or may not be the answer that emerges from your Value Creation Conversations, finding out what value gap or other issues cause customers to leave and fixing it to Regain lost customers will add Top-Line Growth quickly and easily. Leveraging what you've learned from Ramp Up customers drives sales opportunities with new customers, drives opportunities to price for value, and is highly effective for driving Top-Line Growth. Do you want it badly enough to do it?

SOLUTION IN PLAIN SIGHT #3
Sell at Higher Prices, Even in Tough Competitive Markets, Even If You're Skeptical

Safe, subtle, pricing increases are the fastest way to generate Top-Line Growth and Bottom-Line Profit in a hurry. Success stories that clients have shared cite *10-50% bottom-line impact* almost immediately from just *one* of the 21 Safe, Sustainable Ways to Price for Value that many businesses fail to take advantage of. I can assure you that it's very doable even if you're in a tough competitive marketplace. While we can't go into every one of the 21 pricing strategies here, I will get you started and you can access all the others in the Resources for this Chapter.

Now, I know that in tough economic times and low inflation, you can't knock yourself out of the market and hand your business to your competitors by drastically increasing prices, but think about it — haven't the costs that *you* pay to various suppliers gone up in the last while? It's time for you to capture the opportunities you've been missing out on.

Your first step is to establish your customers' willingness-to-pay threshold by understanding what they value about doing business with you. By this time it will come as no surprise when I tell you that you'll be able to do that in your Value Creation Conversations when you use the appropriate willingness-to-pay questions for your quadrant of the Enthused Customer Matrix to learn everything you need to know.

Price is not what we charge; it's what the customer is willing to pay.

Imagine that you're thirsty and there is a water fountain in your office hallway. All you need to do is push the button to get a stream of cool, clear water. How much would you be willing to pay for that water, at that moment? Zero, right? It's there and it's free to you. Now, imagine your car has broken down in the desert and ratchet your thirst up by about 1000%. Can you feel the sun beating down on you and feel your cracked, parched lips? How much would you be willing to pay for that same cool, clear water now? Priceless, right?

In the developed world, water is technically about as commoditized as it gets — and yet we all pay *very* different prices for water, often in the same day, to get exactly the same thing. Branding bottled water has become an art form, all to support price differentiation. Value is in the eye of the beholder — or in the needs and wants of the person buying our product or service — not in how we price it. Whatever your product or service may be, you have an opportunity to price for value with customers whose needs drive a higher willingness-to-pay. Price for the perceived value of your lettuce!

When you use the Value Creation Conversations to understand Who's Who and change behaviors across your organization, you may well find that your marginally profitable blue-chip customers are happy to pay a service charge for extras that better meet their needs. You'll find that many high-maintenance customers all of a sudden don't really need that rush order when there's an added cost *to them* instead of *to you*. Those who genuinely need it will often gladly pay. Take a look at all the little value-add extras that have crept into your systems over time that you're not charging for. The Customer Profitability Diamond helps you overlay optimized pricing *strategically*, as well as tactically. You may well wish to continue to offer those little value-add extras gratis to your highly profitable customers, switch to a billable service for your marginally profitable customers, and offer them as a fee-based service for all new accounts.

You don't have to gouge. You simply have to have the guts to price for benefits perceived by your customers, and for the uncommon value-add that you may not even know you're creating until your customers tell you about the difference it makes to their business.

You'll be able to implement safe, subtle price optimization immediately to drive Top-Line Growth *and* Bottom-Line Profit.

Figure 1: WILLINGNESS-TO-PAY THRESHOLD

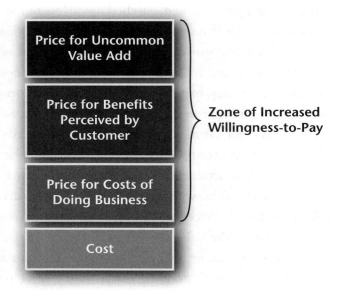

Understanding Willingness-to-Pay Drives Big Impact

When a plastics manufacturer implemented just three of the 21 Safe, Sustainable Ways to Price for Value, he kept his most visible prices highly competitive.

However, he was also able to price for value for less-easily-comparable aftermarket products and follow on services, once he knew which of those were most highly valued by his customers and why. He increased prices between 3 and 6% on a variety of items, saw *no* downturn in volume, increased his Top–Line Growth by *over 40%* and saw a *61% increase* to his bottom line in less than 3 months. Once he understood his customers' willingness-to-pay, he found his lettuce.

His customers became more aware of the value he was bringing to their businesses as a result of the dialogue, which opened up a whole new type of conversation about how to prosper together.

Your Takeaway: Despite being in a highly competitive market, he successfully sold at higher prices.

 Rapid Results Resources: You don't want to guess at what the market will bear. You have to know what gaps and unmet needs a customer has in order to find ways to add value that supports premium pricing. Access "Who Has the Pricing Power" and the "21 Safe, Sustainable Ways to Price for Value" Resources at www.ProfitInPlainSight.com/PriceforValue to get a sense of where your best opportunities for acting on willingness-to-pay exist, given your competitive situation.

Use the Comprehensive Resources — Never Reinvent the Wheel

Leaders who want Top-Line Growth initially struggle to let go of their focus on chasing new customers and new markets and wrestle with how to price for value in competitive markets. It's not their fault; neither they nor their teams have ever been taught that there are highly effective strategies that turbocharge the good things they're already doing.

The good news is that you don't have to choose between new customers and the strategies outlined above. Sales can continue to pursue new business while senior resources conduct Value Creation Conversations and then work with marketing, service, and sales to transform the value-add components and price for value. Your sales team will be the net beneficiaries when you "Find Your Lettuce" and help them sell more, to more customers, at higher prices. It's a win-win all around.

The systematic Profit in Plain Sight Framework provides proven, practical, step-by-step instructions to implement the Ramp Up, Regain, and Reactivate Strategies you've learned, plus a road map to implement up to 21 Safe, Sustainable Ways to Price for Value. Get started with your Rapid Results Resources at *www.ProfitIn PlainSight.com/GetProactive* and *www.ProfitInPlainSight.com/ PriceforValue*.

Summary

A bird in the hand is worth two in the bush. There's a reason this parable makes so much sense in the context of Top-Line Growth.

When you overlook all the birds you already have, you overlook your fastest and easiest opportunities for Top-Line Growth by failing to understand all the different ways you can add value to your customers ... and price for it. There's an opportunity to impact your entire business and accelerate your Top-Line Growth far beyond what any individual customer can generate when you really understand and fulfill needs your customers may not even have thought about, better than anyone else can, such as the membership organization who found a dozen new revenue streams right under their nose.

This isn't a "nice to do" for "someday." You want to take action on this immediately, even if you're on track to achieve the growth objectives you've set. These hidden opportunities simply mean that you've set your growth targets *too low*. The Top-Line Growth you generate will take your business in new directions and that's what transformation is about. You run a business that's a lot more interesting than growing lettuce. If they can do it, you can do it. Find your lettuce. And price for value.

As with all things in business, generating sustained and steady Top-Line Growth is an ongoing process. When you have a steady flow of new customers your organization will tend to take it for granted, but you must always be planning for a rainy day by getting into the habit of generating growth from your *existing* customers. Now you have the tools to do just that.

You can spend a lot of time to figure out how to generate Top-Line Growth in new ways on your own or you can use proven approaches that deliver results.

In this Challenge, you saw how to connect with Retain and Ramp Up customers to add value and sell at higher prices when you understand willingness-to-pay. When you implement these Solutions in Plain Sight on an ongoing basis, you'll almost effortlessly sell more products and services to more customers at higher prices and achieve sustained and steady Top-Line Growth.

Before you implement any significant price increases, you'll test them just to be on the safe side of course with your Restore to Breakeven or Better customers where you have nothing to lose but the red ink. We'll discuss this strategy in Challenge #3: Bottom-Line Growth.

In the meantime, every time you have lettuce on your fork, ask yourself if you've "found the lettuce" in your business. Every time you take a swig of bottled water, ask yourself if you're pricing for perceived value as well as you could be.

This Works. You Can Do It. You Will Succeed.

Take these Actions

Transformation takes more than awareness and good intentions.

Assessment

1. Take 11 minutes to complete the "Profit in Plain Sight Assessment" at *www.ProfitInPlainSight.com/Profit* and pass the link along to your team so that you can compare notes.

2. Access "Who Has the Pricing Power" and the "21 Safe, Sustainable Ways to Price for Value" Resources at *www.ProfitInPlainSight.com/PriceforValue* to get a sense of where your best opportunities for acting on willingness-to-pay exist, given your competitive situation.

Resource

3. Transform your Value Creation Conversations into Top-Line impact at *www.ProfitInPlainSight.com/GetProactive*.

Action Item

4. Schedule a team meeting to:
   - Ask the Tough Love questions from the beginning of this Chapter.
   - Hold each other accountable when you hear tethered language or observe left-brain-dominated thinking.
   - Review your "Profit in Plain Sight Assessment" results and compare notes.
   - Implement the Profit and Growth Accelerators from the Resource links above.
   - Start looking for your lettuce, everywhere in your business. Need help? The "Find Your Lettuce" topic makes a great keynote at your industry conference or your annual sales meeting. Itching to get started? Schedule a webinar that will reach everyone on your sales

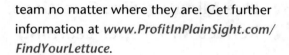

team no matter where they are. Get further information at *www.ProfitInPlainSight.com/ FindYourLettuce.*

Small Steps. Big Impact!

Five Minutes, Five Questions: Reflect for Deeper Learning

Your first step is *internal* transformation, to identify what attitudes have already shifted and what behaviors will follow.

1. What ideas immediately came to mind when I considered the "Lettuce" Strategy to Ramp Up customers in our business?

2. What was my initial reaction to the Regain Strategy and the value of going back to lost customers? Was it reluctance or dread? If so, what is my greatest concern over what we might hear?

3. Have we accepted pricing increases from suppliers that are larger than those we've applied to our products and services over the past few years? If so, why is there that gap?

4. Does my discomfort in passing along price increases reflect my perception that we don't offer enough value to support charging more, or am I simply tethered, assuming that our customers are unwilling to pay more, instead of fully understanding their willingness-to-pay?

5. How do the solutions proposed for Top-Line Growth outweigh any resistance I anticipate from others on our team to focus on opportunities *within* our customer base, rather than focusing on new business from new customers?

Inform. Inspire. Motivate. Transform.
Infuse. Enthuse.

Ensuring Bottom-Line Growth in Profit

Stop Vampire Customers from Sucking the Lifeblood Out of Your Business

Vampires may be popular in the movies, but they don't belong in your business.

PRACTICAL SOLUTIONS ENTHUSE YOUR CUSTOMERS

SOLUTIONS: 5 Rs for Proactively Managing Customer Profitability

Challenge #3 Bottom-Line Growth

What would it be like not only to know which customers you're losing money on, but to be able to help them become profitable again almost immediately so that you don't have to fire them and take a hit to your volume or top line?

How much time and effort could be saved in your business if you could proactively spot the customers who are likely to cost you more than they're worth and take action before they become a problem?

What could you accomplish in your business if you could proactively manage customer profitability on an ongoing basis, in significantly less time than you're spending on e-mail?

I was struck by the differences in the stories two executives shared at a seminar. One was a senior manager at a molded plastics firm who told me that his company knew they were losing money on every single first order because that was "the way their industry worked," hoping to make up the loss on future orders. The company was in receivership and he was looking for a new job.

The CEO of a high-end office paper recycling business had a different story. Her company was picking up paper from a customer's office, shredding it, pulping it, and reselling the recycled product. The problem was they were essentially offering a high-end janitorial service for less than $50 per month, which was simply not sustainable. She decided to take the bull by the horns and told the customer that, effective immediately, the new monthly rate would be $300, because she knew that taking the chance of losing the customer was better than continually losing money on them.

When I ask seminar attendees what they think happened next, most shake their heads and say something along the lines of "The customer told the recycling company where to go." What the customer actually said was, "What took you so long?" and paid the new price with no problem. The business relationship was solid, he'd been receiving unsolicited competitive quotes, and he knew exactly how good a deal he had. All of that new revenue fell straight to the bottom line.

Both executives were the victims of self-inflicted wounds. The senior manager allowed his bottom line to be continually sucked dry by Vampire Customers, while the CEO had initially failed to price for profit, but took the risk to confront the problem head-on and find a solution. Now, of course, there are a whole range of options between these extremes.

Growth in Profit Is for You When ...

... you instinctively know that you're losing money on some customers, but have yet to find an effective way to deal with them;

... you don't want to fire unprofitable customers, because your business needs their volume to cover fixed costs; and

... you want to find an effective way to spot potential Vampires early, before they can do any damage to your bottom line.

Slowly but surely you've already been discovering the 5Rs embedded in the Proactively Managing Customer Profitability element of the systematic Profit in Plain Sight Framework: Retain, Ramp Up, Restore, Regain, and Reactivate. We highlighted the first two — Retain, and Ramp Up in Challenge #2 (Top-Line Growth), and focused on just one of the seven components of the Ramp Up Strategy — selling more products and services using the "lettuce" approach. We layered in the fourth R — selling to more customers by Regaining lost customers, and touched briefly on the benefits of Reactivating dormant customers.

In this Chapter, you'll master a critical R that you discovered when you first constructed your Customer Profitability Diamond — Restore unprofitable customers to Breakeven or Better and ensure Bottom-Line Growth in Profit. You'll learn how to deal with any self-inflicted wounds that are turning perfectly good customers into Vampires as a taste of what's to come in Challenge #4, Developing a Corporate Reputation for Quality, and how to deal with customers whose own bad behaviors are making them a nightmare for you. Then, you'll develop specific low-cost, low-effort, beyond-breakeven strategies to help unprofitable customers either add profits to your bottom line or exit gracefully. Your bottom line will start looking very healthy rather than anemic.

Finally you'll have what you need to build cost-effective and impactful sales-service plans to reflect the level of investment that's appropriate for every customer group, or even individual customers, and that leverages everything you've learned from the 5Rs. Your plan will reflect your customers' wants and needs, not simply well-intentioned *best guesses*. Some customers will benefit from less marketing and more value-add communications or services. Others don't need the costly extras, they just need value-add sales efforts on a schedule that works for their buying cycles.

Most companies get this completely backwards, spending sales dollars when they should be spending service dollars and spending service dollars when they should be spending sales dollars. All of your choices impact your Growth in your Bottom-Line Profit.

Tough Love: Ask Your Leadership Team Five Critical Questions

1. How aware are all of our managers and front-line people of which customers we are losing money on and how much they're costing us?

2. How proactive and effective are we today at restoring them to profitability or do we more often ignore the situation and hope it will resolve itself?

3. How effective are we at gracefully firing a customer when that's the right thing to do or do we leave a trail of hard feelings and negative word of mouth?

4. How much longer are we prepared to let unprofitable customers steal our hard-earned bottom line from us, when that money could be better spent on growing our own business?

5. How open are we to taking a hit in revenue and volume as a worst-case scenario while we potentially transition unprofitable customers up or out, as long as our bottom line is improving as a result?

 Rapid Results Resources: If you haven't yet taken action to construct your Customer Profitability Diamond, you'll find it essential for taking advantage of the Solutions to the Challenge of Bottom-Line Growth in Profit. Access your Rapid Results Resources at www.ProfitIn PlainSight.com/GetInsights.

Keep untethering as we expose a few myths surrounding unprofitable customers.

 ## Move Beyond the Myths

Which of these three myths are preventing you from ensuring Bottom-Line Growth in Profit?

 ### MYTH #1
Cutting Costs Is the Key to Profitability

FACT: You can't shrink your way to growth and most of us were taught to cut costs the wrong way. We cut training, travel, expenses, hiring, perks, and key investments — all of which are actually expenditures contributing to the future of our business. However, cutting the costs that hold us back from our future — unprofitable customers — is a much more impactful and intelligent strategy.

FACT: Have you ever bent over backwards to try to keep a challenging customer happy and inadvertently ratcheted up your sales and service costs as a result? Have you ever lost a good sales, service, or accounts receivable person because customer demands or abusive behavior finally took too much of a toll? You want to eliminate the *hidden costs* of over-servicing, low morale, and demotivation that are often caused by the kinds of behaviors exhibited by Vampire Customers.

 ### MYTH #2
Fire the Customer!

We've all been taught that the easiest fix to this dilemma is to fire the customer! You'll see six scenarios that can result in an unprofitable customer later in this Chapter, and how in five out of those six scenarios, firing the customer is exactly the *wrong* thing to do.

FACT: Often our customers are unprofitable because of our own self-inflicted wounds — pricing, terms, or service issues of our own making. It's our responsibility to clean up our own house first and find ways to serve them at a profit.

FACT: Often our customers are unprofitable because of their own behaviors such as only purchasing less-profitable components of our product mix or poor payment history. We can guide them to more profitable behaviors instead.

FACT: Often firing customers indiscriminately will simply spread a larger share of fixed costs to profitable customers ... and make them technically unprofitable. Carry on with the "fire the customer" strategy on that basis and you'll be out of business in no time.

FACT: Some of our technically unprofitable customers may be our biggest fans, sending us referral business or providing testimonials that help us secure new and profitable business.

MYTH #3
Vampire Customers Will Leave If We Raise Prices

FACT: Look what our recycling CEO would have given up if she'd simply taken that approach. Often our customers know that they're not profitable for us. Well, even if they leave (and some will) when you raise prices, it's still a win for you, because you've stopped the bleeding. Let your competitors bleed red ink instead. Often customers are open to a "let's make this work" conversation. By way of a parallel, have you ever agonized over firing an employee and delayed it as long as you could, only to find that it was no surprise to them? We often put off the difficult customer conversations, but when we know why the lack of profitability is occurring and have constructive ideas on how to address the problem, customers are often open to listening.

Expand Your Thinking to Close the Gaps
The True Cost of Vampire Customers

Costly Vampire Customers are all too easy to overlook because, unlike "nightmare customers," it is not always bad behaviors on their part that are the problem. The challenge is to spot the Vampire Customers who are under the radar. Most often you're going to find that their Vampire status is not a result of *their* behavior but of what's going on within your own company — it's a self-inflicted wound. Here's why.

GAP #1
It Takes Two to Tango

Do you know someone who has been divorced? Did they start out in love? Was it ever really just the fault of one of them that the marriage ended? Profitable customers sometimes free-fall into becoming Vampire Customers in exactly the same way.

Unless you're selling loss-leader business, every customer technically starts out profitable. What happens? Over time, either their bad behavior or our poor management of the costs of sales and service changes the equation until we can't wait to end the relationship. But, they're still providing volume that we need, to keep our costs manageable. Or they're a blue-chip account and it would give us a black eye in the industry if we lost them. So we put up with lack of profitability. It's not a marriage made in heaven, but we've never been taught how to fix it. It's time to get some professional counseling by looking at alternative scenarios before you throw in the towel.

In the Customer Profitability Diamond, you identified *qualitative* reasons why customers are unprofitable for you. If you've been relying purely on accounting measures to identify unprofitable customers, you're overlooking factors that will never turn up on a spreadsheet and losing out on the opportunity to close that gap. This is why the *qualitative* approach of the Customer Profitability Diamond is so valuable.

Figure 1: **CUSTOMER PROFITABILITY DIAMOND**

Restore to Breakeven or Better

Shining a Light on the Vampires

A large valve manufacturing company found that almost every time they grew revenues, they seemed to dig themselves into a deeper hole on their bottom line. When they took the time to get to the bottom of the mystery of the lost revenues, they found they were losing money on *28%* of their customers.

When they calculated just how much that was costing them, they found that it was the same as writing a check for $75,000.00 *every month.*

You're writing a check too, you simply may not know the amount. You simply cannot ensure or maintain Bottom-Line Growth if that much life-blood is being sucked from your business.

Your Takeaway: Do you know how big of a check you're writing every month?

GAP #2
Firing Your Customers Is Not Your Only Option

Most of us are justifiably reluctant to fire our customers. When you have other highly effective alternatives, it becomes much easier to take action. Don't lose out on opportunities to close this gap because you're tethered to conventional thinking.

Rebalance Value

We've all been taught not to lose a customer. Many of your people are probably bending over backwards to keep your most demanding customers, thinking they're doing the right thing.

In fact, they're just making the problem worse until you share with them how those customers are putting your business at risk. You want to close this gap as quickly as possible with a proven wake-up call using the Who's Who Customer Profitability Diamond.

It doesn't necessarily mean firing them, it just means a rebalancing of how value is given and received in the relationship with the right level of sales and service.

Your Takeaway: You don't have to lose essential business volume when you get proactive with Vampire Customers.

GAP #3
Reluctance to Lose the Red Ink

You want to help everyone in your organization come to the realization that you lose *absolutely nothing but the red ink* if an unprofitable customer leaves due to pricing increases, so don't be shy about testing price changes on this group.

The Grass Isn't Always Greener

Customers often find that the grass is *not* greener elsewhere even if they initially get a cheaper price from one of your competitors.

As long as you have gracefully left the door open, there is no reason why they won't return ... at higher prices. Don't keep sabotaging your Bottom-Line Growth in Profit when you could be closing this gap with strategic pricing.

Your Takeaway: Always leave the door open, and price for value and profit.

Consequences
The Blood-Sucking Costs of Business as Usual

It's time to get very passionate about taking back what's yours, instead of writing checks to your Vampires! Taking action on unprofitable customers is risky if you just assume they should all be fired. But it's actually not very onerous when you approach it in a constructive way, and in fact you'll create a tremendous feel-good when you simply get this nagging issue off your plate.

Taking action to figure out and fix the reasons customers are costing you money might seem like a "nice to do" but who's got time for that? *You* do, if you have time to do e-mail every day. It will have a return on investment many, many times what you get from spending time on e-mail and will take no longer than that to turn it around. You want to stop the bleeding *now*. All of those checks that you're writing to your customers simply for the value *they* receive from doing business with *you* should be checks you write to yourself, to your employees, and to your business in recognition of the hard work and time that you're all investing. Every unprofitable customer is draining time and energy out of your organization that you could be spending to add value to new and existing customers. It's simply not an acceptable business practice to continue to ignore this critical customer group.

Tourniquet for Cash

When the CEO of a construction company stopped the bleeding with his Vampire Customers, he found that he finally had the cash to hire an estimating engineer, a new hire that he'd been putting on hold for over a year. The estimating engineer was able to fine-tune the quotes for higher profits, the company won more business, and the CEO finally had the time to get more strategic in his business.

Your Takeaway: What are you putting on hold because you haven't stopped the bleeding?

Every time you sign a check on behalf of your business or in your personal life, regardless of who it's made out to, I want you to imagine that it's made out to one of your Vampire Customers instead. I want you to lose sleep wondering what all those Vampire Customer checks really add up to over the course of the year and how much those customers are stealing from your business every day that you delay doing something about it. What they're stealing is more than money. It's your dreams, your investments in your business, your security, and that of all those who work in your company. And you're letting it happen, until you have an effective system for doing something different. You deserve more for your efforts, don't you? Take simple steps to transform bleeding into Bottom-Line Growth in Profits.

> *Rapid Results Resources:* A great first step is simply to stop the profit leaks that are preventing all the hard work you do to build your Top–Line Growth from ever showing up on your Bottom Line. Find out how to do that at www.ProfitInPlainSight.com/GetProactive.

Solutions in Plain Sight
Write Checks to Your Business,
Not to Your Vampires

Imagine how valuable it will be to Restore your Vampire Customers to Breakeven or Better so that you can write checks for those things on your Blue Sky Bucket List of investments you would make in your business if only you had the Bottom-Line Growth in Profits to do it.

Imagine how valuable it will be to finally have sales-service plans that reflect the level of investment that makes sense for each customer or group of customers.

Many leaders fail to have the right information to make smart choices before taking action on unprofitable customers. Assumptions are made about customers that may or may not be based on fact. Salespeople are left out of being part of the solution and get demotivated when they see what they think of as the fruits of their labor being discarded when decisions are made to fire the customer (the Revenue Trap, again). While I can't go into all of the nuances of the conversations that need to happen about compensation and next steps within this book, I can share with you three simple Solutions in Plain Sight that will get you started.

SOLUTION IN PLAIN SIGHT #1

Determine Who's Worth Saving and Who Should Be Exited Gracefully

Some customers are worth saving, some are not, based on which of the six scenarios they fall into (see Figure 2). Would you want to have different strategies for a customer who is technically unprofitable because you've underpriced your products or are over-delivering on service versus a high-maintenance customer who demands you rework every time they change their mind and never pay their bills on time? Of course you would! One unprofitable customer is a result of your own self-inflicted wounds. One is due to their own bad behavior. That's why "fire the customer" is not always the right answer.

Figure 2: SIX SCENARIOS OF UNPROFITABLE CUSTOMERS

	Source of the Profitability Problem Is *Us*: it's a self-inflicted wound *Example: Loss-leader pricing or bend-over backwards service*	Source of the Profitability Problem Is *Them*: it's bad behavior on their part *Example: Unnecessary re-work requests or late payment*
They're fans of ours	Make it right immediately	Have a "How do we make this work" conversation
They're neutral towards us	Fix and make-up	Have a "We love you too but ..." conversation
They're unfriendlies due to inertia or feeling trapped	Fix at the lowest cost possible	Fire them gracefully

You'll need to have some internal conversations about the merits of focusing on profit versus revenue to get this process started and eliminate resistance, especially if you measure and reward individuals on the basis of revenue. As you sort out your unprofitable customers, it may be that revenues will temporarily go *down* as profits go *up*.

You may find that you need to shift gears on compensation to drive the right behaviors, because revenue-based compensation tends to strip profitability out of the equation. Some clients move to a gross margin basis, others bonus based on profitability, others implement profit-sharing methods. To a large degree it depends on the type of business you're in and what level of number-crunching is supported, but don't overlook this crucial component.

You'll get what you incent, so if Bottom-Line Growth in Profit is your objective, your incentive plans need to reflect that.

I advise my clients to implement a very *abbreviated* version of the Value Creation Conversation with this customer group. Once you know *why* a customer is in your unprofitable segment, and whether or not they are loyal to you or not, you can develop an appropriate action plan to Restore them to Breakeven or Better or exit them gracefully.

These customers are already costing you money and the last thing you want to do is invest in them further until you know if it's justified.

Too many organizations who attempt this on their own inadvertently complicate it by adding conventional customer satisfaction questions or try to automate this with a survey. You want to be voice-to-voice briefly on this one, as you really want 100% participation and candid feedback.

Implementing a Restore to Breakeven or Better action plan is a great way to develop a junior member of your team and help them make solid recommendations on what actions to implement. Once you have clarity on next steps, you can determine who on the team needs to contact each customer.

Win-Win Solution

When a service provider decided to get serious about customer profitability and targeted 400 platinum clients for special retention efforts, they increased their revenues with *that group* by 54%. Meanwhile, they exited unprofitable clients from the rest of their client base.

Although *overall revenues* for their client base that year went down 4% as a result, operating profits *went up* 12% and shareholder value *doubled*. They advised all stakeholders in advance of the anticipated revenue drop so that everyone was prepared for it, but it turned out to be smaller than anticipated. They switched their compensation system from one that was revenue-based to profit sharing. Everybody won.

Would you accept a decline in revenue for those types of bottom-line results?

Your Takeaway: It's not about revenue. It's about profit.

 Rapid Results Resources: Access everything you need to help you implement your back to Breakeven or Better Strategy more quickly and easily at www.ProfitInPlainSight.com/GetProactive.

 SOLUTION IN PLAIN SIGHT #2
Keep Some Garlic on Hand for the Vampires

Determining who is unprofitable from a *qualitative* aspect when you construct your Customer Profitability Diamond is not an exact science as noted earlier, nor should it be.

Your Who's Who of customers will change over time, that is,

some customers may start negotiating aggressively due to market changes and your sales team may slip into selling price instead of value to keep the revenue numbers on track. Or the customer may become high maintenance in a variety of ways and your service people try to do the right thing by bending over backwards. There are a myriad of reasons, but the point is that customer behavior is *always* changing.

When the problem is bad behavior on the part of the customer, what's required is immediate action to change that. Some customers will always grind on price, some will always be overly demanding. That's OK. A relationship based on mutual wins and value is not for everyone. Your Customer Profitability Diamond creates an early warning system that provides input to make good decisions and dynamically manage unprofitable behaviors, because all of those qualitative factors are observable. Have your sales and service folks start to keep an eye out for early indicators of future bad behavior and actively implement the following garlic strategies:

- stipulate extended delivery times;
- indicate that you cannot meet the required specifications;
- set your price for profit to test the customers' Willingness-to-Pay;
- deliberately price yourself out of the market; or
- recommend another supplier who may better fit their needs.

The customer either fires themselves or becomes profitable again! But they make the call that's right for them.

Always leave the door open for them to come back on different terms that are more advantageous to you, even if a "you're fired!" approach would feel more satisfying. That's the biggest challenge I see with companies who latch onto the Restore strategy but implement it without taking the time to really understand it. Making a customer *feel* fired should always be the last resort. You never want to create a backlash that can spread by word of mouth in your industry. Subtle, effective solutions are the way to go.

When you can easily spot a customer who is going bad or spot self-inflicted wounds before they become a major issue, proactively managing the Customer Profitability Ratio becomes play instead of work and is a sustainable way of ensuring healthy Bottom-Line Growth in Profit.

The Fine Art of Firing the Customer

A custom machine shop has the art of firing a customer down to a fine art ... and it often happens *before* a prospect even becomes a customer!

They have identified the specific profiles of customers who are likely to be profitable and those who aren't. When a potentially unprofitable customer asks for a quote, they cheerfully provide a "priced-for-generous-profit" version and also provide the names of less expensive competitors. They position themselves in their market as experts in high-end, value-add business, not run-of-the-mill machining that anyone can do.

And ... you guessed it, the would-be customers usually go looking for other quotes and buy their low-margin business from the "cheaper" competition. Some have no objection to the "priced-for-generous-profit" quote and become customers. Many of those potential customers who initially choose the less-costly competitor return and become customers for higher-end, more profitable business, which is exactly the niche this machine shop wants and has gently trained their customers to buy from them.

In every case they create a win for their company and a win for their customer. The big takeaway is that this company "fires" potential unprofitable customers long before they have the chance to damage the bottom line. They actually earn trust and credibility when the "fired" customer spreads positive word of mouth at trade shows on how the custom machine shop saved them money by recommending a competitor!

Your Takeaway: These conversations don't have to be awkward at all!

SOLUTION IN PLAIN SIGHT #3
Develop Your Sales-Service Plans

One of the greatest takeaways from exploring each of the 5Rs for Proactively Managing Customer Profitability is to have a very clear sense of what you need to do next to proactively manage customer profitability, including the scenarios listed below.

- Which customers are already doing as much business with you as they can … and may benefit from investments in servicing their account in ways that add value to promote retention, rather than continued conventional sales efforts.

- Which customers have the potential to do more business with you … and would benefit from a higher level of value-add sales investments to demonstrate how you can save them time, save or make them money, solve the problems they're wrestling with, provide peace of mind, or make them feel good.

- Which customers have ended up over time being serviced at a high level to the extent that they are only marginally profitable or even unprofitable … and would benefit from re-thinking how to serve them in more cost-effective ways or price for value so that the relationship can continue.

- Which customers have left you, but would return to do more business again when you resolve the reasons they left ... which will also impact how well you retain existing customers, and which may even impact your understanding of what the real value proposition is for new prospects.

- Which customers are inactive, and why ... so that you can reach out to them in value-add ways to renew the relationship and be a valued supplier to them.

Once you drill down into your Who's Who with your Value Creation Conversations, you'll have a very good sense of which customers you want to grow, which you want to maintain at status quo, and which you may even want to do less business with — because it's not just about generating revenue, it's about generating profitable revenue. Unlike the unfortunate manager who inherited his sales team of "good ol' boys" who indiscriminately took every client out for golf and lunches regardless of their value to the company, you can develop Sales-Service Plans that reflect what you can afford to invest in your clients, and how you can do it in a strategic way that adds value to the relationship for them.

The Hidden Value of the Right Sales-Service Plan

A high-tech manufacturer insisted on sending out a large glossy catalog annually plus individual flyers weekly to its entire mailing list. They mailed everything to everyone, regardless of the individual's interests or how long it had been since they purchased anything. Needless to say, that caused some challenges with profitability!

When they implemented the Restore to Breakeven or Better Value Creation Conversation with one customer in particular, they found that many of the mailings were *never even reaching* their decision-makers' desks. There were so many names from that client company on the mailing list that marketing materials were arriving on pallets and were not even being broken down by mail room staff, let alone delivered or returned as undeliverable! It turned out that many of the people on the mailing list were no longer with that company, but that those who were still there had largely stopped buying because they "never heard from the supplier!"

Imagine if the supplier had never taken steps to understand what was going on with this Vampire Customer.

When they cleaned up their self-inflicted wound, they reduced catalog production and mailing costs by 50% and increased margins by 5% using more effective and less costly ways to reach those so-called Vampire Customers. Both parties were responsible for the almost-divorce: my client had created a self-inflicted wound with excessive mailings and their customer was guilty of neither delivering what they saw as junk mail to their employees nor letting their supplier know that it was unwelcome. If my client had simply fired the customer indiscriminately, they would have forgone significant (and eventually profitable) business.

Your Takeaway: Taking the bull by the horns will strengthen the relationship.

Developing sales-service plans that enable you to create a process of proactively managing customer profitability and invest wisely to create value in your customer relationships doesn't have to be onerous or time-consuming. It just has to be a dynamic process that you rebalance periodically and simply implement as an ongoing way of doing business. With a clear understanding of your 5Rs in your customer base, the answers you've been seeking will be right in Plain Sight.

Rapid Results Resources: When you're ready to develop highly effective sales-service plans to proactively manage customer profitability on an ongoing basis, access the resources to help you do that at www.ProfitInPlainSight.com/GetProactive.

Use the Comprehensive Resources — Never Reinvent the Wheel

One of the biggest challenges I see is that the issue of unprofitable customers simply isn't made visible within the organization. It's something taken for granted, just like knowing that half of any marketing budget is being wasted — but just not knowing which half.

The other big challenge is that none of us were ever taught to ask the right questions and develop good strategies that we could implement without cringing. Stop staying stuck. This is about transformation and you can't get there by doing what you've done to date. You've just seen the effective alternatives that are available to you. You have three choices.

1. Continue to ignore Vampire Customers.

2. Use conventional approaches to fire them all and risk losing the volumes that are contributing to overhead.

3. Use a practical, proven approach that offers effective solutions to eliminate the problem by creating clarity on what has caused the customer to become a Vampire.

You're seeing how the systematic Profit in Plain Sight Framework builds proactive customer profitability management strategies step by step, from shining a spotlight on the Customer Profitability

Ratio, to generating deep insights with the Value Creation Conversations, to systematically implementing the 5Rs for Proactively Managing Customer Profitability (Retain, Ramp Up, Regain, Reactivate, Restore to Breakeven or Better), to turning good information into great Customer Retention and Loyalty, Top-Line Growth and Bottom–Line Growth in Profits.

This foundational work holds the key to solving your two remaining Challenges: Building a Corporate Reputation for Quality and Stimulating Innovation and Creativity and Enabling Entrepreneurship.

All you lack are the integrated resources to make it happen more quickly and easily without reinventing the wheel.

Summary

Vampires only thrive in the dark and as long as you're in the dark on customer profitability, you're vulnerable. They cost you your Bottom-Line Growth in Profit and they cost you your dreams by stealing the money that you could be investing to move your company to a new level.

This isn't a "nice to do someday." You want to take action on this immediately, even if you're satisfied with your profits today. Dealing with Vampire Customers will take a load off of everyone in the organization and that's part of what an effective transformation does. You want to take back those checks you've been writing and put them in your own bank account instead of into your customers' hands.

As with all things in business, dealing with your unprofitable customers requires clarity to make the right decisions and time well spent to implement solutions. You can spend a lot of time figuring out the most effective approaches on your own or you can use proven approaches that deliver results.

When you systematically work through the Restore to Breakeven or Better strategies you'll not only deal constructively with today's

Vampires and get them back on track, but you'll proactively catch unprofitable behaviors before they can damage your bottom line in the future. You'll stop the bleeding, enhance profitability and growth, and fully reignite the Passion in your organization when you gracefully fire customers who are making your employees' lives miserable. You'll reap the rewards of the value you and your employees have created for your customers. Bottom-Line Growth in Profit is an immediate outcome of dealing with your Vampires and provides the foundation for ongoing investments to further differentiate from your competition and help your customers do what they need to do better.

This Works. You Can Do It. You Will Succeed.

Take these Actions

Transformation takes more than awareness and good intentions.

Assessment	**1.** Take 11 minutes to complete the "Profit in Plain Sight Assessment" at *www.ProfitInPlainSight. com/Profit* and pass the link along to your team so that you can compare notes.
Resource	**2.** If you haven't yet taken action to construct your Customer Profitability Diamond, you'll find it essential for taking advantage of the Solutions to the Challenge of Bottom-Line Growth in Profit. Access your Rapid Results Resources at *www.ProfitInPlainSight.com/GetInsights*.
Resource	**3.** Take action immediately to stop the leaks that are preventing all the hard work that you do to build your Top Line from ever appearing on your Bottom Line. Get started at *www.ProfitInPlain Sight.com/GetProactive*.
Action Item	**4.** Schedule a team meeting to: • Ask the Tough Love questions from the beginning of this Chapter. • Hold each other accountable when you hear tethered language or observe left-brain-dominated thinking regarding unprofitable customers. • Review your "Profit in Plain Sight Assessment" results. • Start to have the internal conversations regarding the implications of short-term dips in Revenue and volume if firing a customer turns out to be the right strategy in some cases.

- Implement your Rapid Results Resources to Restore your customers to Breakeven or Better and build your sales-service plans.

Small Steps. Big Impact!

Five Minutes, Five Questions: Reflect for Deeper Learning

Your first step is *internal* transformation, to identify what attitudes have already shifted and what behaviors will follow.

1. How has my resolution to address the issue of Vampires in our business taken shape as I've reviewed the implications and how-tos?

   _____

2. How has the concept of "them" versus "us" (bad customer behaviors versus self-inflicted wounds as a factor in profitability) changed my perceptions of when it's time to fire a customer?

   _____

3. What are the internal conversations I'll need to have so that we can plan for a potential decrease in revenues in the short term, even as profits increase?

   _____

4. What are the most significant issues or opportunities I anticipate when developing sales-service plans that will help us proactively manage customer profitability?

   _____

5. What is the best-case (yes, best) scenario of allowing Vampire Customers to *continue* sucking the lifeblood out of our business? What is my worst-case scenario of proactively *dealing with* unprofitable customers?

   _____

Inform. Inspire. Motivate. Transform.
Infuse. Enthuse.

Developing a Corporate Reputation for Quality

Don't Just Oil the Tinman, Make Him Sing and Dance

Simply get it right the first time and, if you don't, make it right the second time.

SOLUTIONS:
3 Uncommon Ways to Eliminate Unnecessary Costs-to-Serve

Challenge #4
Reputation for Quality

How would your market react if they simply found every aspect of doing business with your company so easy and so enjoyable, in ways that they can't quite put their finger on, that you became the gold standard against which all others are measured?

> **What impact would it have on your culture** if all the time your customer service group currently spends fixing things that have gone wrong was instead redirected to value-add activities?
>
> **What would be possible** for your business if you eliminated all the costs of fixing self-inflicted wounds by getting it right the first time?

Remember the Tinman in the *Wizard of Oz*? When Dorothy initially found him, he was rusted solid, unable to move and not of much help to anyone. Oil transformed him from being creaky into the singing, dancing Tinman we all enjoyed so much. Over time, corrosion and creakiness creeps into every business and it needs to be oiled.

When you think of the customer service interactions you have with various suppliers in your personal and business life, how many of them are on the creaky and rusted end of the scale versus the well-oiled end?

How do your customers perceive *your* Quality and your customer service organization when things go awry?

A Reputation for Quality Is for You When ...

... your customer service team tries to get customers off the phone quickly because they're already busy;

... it takes multiple calls or escalation to a manager to resolve many of your incoming service calls; and

... you frequently have to offer compensation to keep a customer happy or discount to regain business you've lost after a customer service incident.

In developing a Reputation for Quality you'll learn how you can leverage the hidden factor of the Quality Equation: Experiential Quality (EQ). Especially if you're already using some form of conventional quality management, you'll find uncommon approaches here that are neither cost- nor labor-intensive, yet deliver tremendous improvements to the Customer Experience, strip Unnecessary-Costs-to-Serve out of your business, and help you build a Reputation for Quality that delivers competitive advantage.

Tough Love: Ask Your Leadership Team Five Critical Questions

1. How do our customers define their need for overall Perceived Quality — not just Functional Quality, but Experiential Quality factors such as reliability, responsiveness, seamlessness, speed, and ease of transaction?

2. Who is the gold standard in our industry today, not just on Functional Quality, but on Experiential Quality and why?

3. Are we above, below, or right at the Quality level required by our customers, and how does that contribute to the value proposition we convey to them?

4. How much time and effort have we invested to make every aspect of our customers' Experiences exceed their expectations or surprise them in good and unexpected ways?

5. Would our customers say their Experiences with us are bad, bland, or great? Are we guessing or do we know for sure?

Rapid Results Resources: Find out how you can take immediate action on five factors that are causing 80% of your service costs at www.ProfitIn PlainSight.com/DeliverQuality.

Keep getting untethered as we expose some common quality myths.

Move Beyond the Myths

Which of these three myths are preventing you from truly achieving a Reputation for Quality?

MYTH #1
Quality Is Product Related and Six Sigma[1] Is the Goal

FACT: Product or service quality is important and Six Sigma is a great end goal in some cases, but it's not appropriate or even desirable for all companies to pursue. Would you pay for Six Sigma quality if you were a bar owner buying paper drink umbrellas to perch in a piña colada?

Functional Quality across most industries is adequate, yet gaining traction on Perceived Quality remains elusive. Perception of Quality is experience-related and begins from the moment the customer finds out about your product or service, right through the purchase and use process, including issue resolution, end-of-life disposal, and repurchase. Every interaction with your firm either helps or hinders your Reputation for Quality, far beyond the product or service quality you provide.

---

[1] *Six Sigma was first developed by Motorola in 1986 but later became well known through Jack Welch's adoption of it as the quality standard at General Electric. Most successful companies have an average of 35,000 defects per million; Six Sigma sets a goal of just 3.4 defects per million.*

MYTH #2
Achieving Sustainable Quality Standards Is Daunting to Measure and Complex to Accomplish

FACT: Complex models have been built around what it takes to deliver total Quality. However, research also shows that just a few factors account for 80% of service-related issues — an important part of the Experience. So you can waste a lot of time trying to get everything perfect or you can have significant impact when you work the 80-20 rule and focus on what customers are really noticing and objecting to. The most common factors are self-inflicted wounds — areas where a failure by the *company* has caused the problem.

MYTH #3
Customer Satisfaction Scores Are a Good Measure of Quality

FACT: Customer satisfaction scores are actually a poor measure of quality, as they don't examine the initial customer expectations or any gaps that may have occurred. If expectations are *low*, you may get a *good* score even with poor quality. If expectations are *high*, you may get a *low* score, even with good quality. And you can't control expectations — they may vary every time the customer experiences your product or service. Early cell-phone users expected dropped calls. Today, flawless wireless almost everywhere is the expectation.

Expand Your Thinking to Close the Gaps
There's More to Quality than What You're Doing Today

With years of quality initiatives behind us, including TQM, Six Sigma, and Lean,[2] Functional Quality has become simply a ticket to entry — most of the products and services we buy work as promised. When we get a lemon, 99% of the time the issue is eventually fixed to our satisfaction.

So why are there still so many disgruntled customers? Why are customer service departments expanding or adding web chat and other alternatives to the traditional phone, fax, and mail/e-mail? Why are companies hiring people to monitor social media for negative mentions about their company?

GAP #1
There's a Bigger Picture to Consider Beyond Functional Quality

Think of the suppliers you use in your personal life that you love to hate or the horror stories of customer service that often come up in casual conversation. Why are there so many glitches in something that should be straightforward? For most of us, our wireless provider, our banks, and the airlines we fly will be in the top five horror-story sources pretty consistently. But is there really a quality problem? If your phone works, if you can get money from the ATM, and if landings equal takeoffs, then the Functional Quality of the product is not the major issue.

Most of us hate those institutions because the Quality of the *Experience* is so dreadful. Our emotional right brain reacts strongly when the vendors we deal with leave a bad taste in our mouths.

---

[2] *Lean principles were derived from the Japanese manufacturing industry but the phrase was coined by John Krafcik in his 1988 article, "Triumph of the Lean Production System," based on his master's thesis and experience as a quality engineer at Toyota-GM. Krafcik is currently the CEO of Hyundai.*

Is It the Product or the Experience that's the Problem?

Quick, think of an unpleasant transaction or interaction you've experienced recently in your personal or business life. For many of us, the Experience of procuring, using, and disposing of the products and services we buy or getting an efficient and effective resolution to any Functional Quality issue is really the "quality" problem.

Long wait times on hold. Needing to repeat the issue over and over again as it's escalated. Long wait times before a solution is found and the need to constantly follow up. Begrudging behaviors on the part of apathetic customer service staff. The Tinman of customer service is not just creaky, he's rusty, corroded, and seized up most of the time.

Customers are usually willing to give a company a second chance when something goes awry, knowing that nobody is perfect. But when the cure is worse than the disease, the negative echoes of the Experience cause many customers to vote with their feet and their wallet the next time.

What are your customers thinking about you, based on what they Experience?

Your Takeaway: When you get the Experience right, you enhance your Reputation for Quality.

GAP #2
Many of the Customer Experiences We Have Every Day Are Simply Bland and Unmemorable

When they are, the opportunity to build brand loyalty is lost.

Try this with your team. Have them list every interaction they have in a single day as a prospect or customer in their personal life.

Have each person rate their Experiences as good, bland, or bad. Then, go around the table and have everyone go through their lists. You'll probably find that many interactions were forgotten altogether until prompted by someone else. Those are the ones that are so bland that they don't even register. If a customer doesn't remember interacting with your brand whether live and in person, on the phone, via snail mail, through an e-mail, or on a website, all the brand value you may have spent millions to build and advertise is completely lost.

Most of us would struggle to think of more than one company in our business or personal lives that creates such amazing Experiences that we simply would never consider another option. But maybe you can think of a supplier who's simply a pleasure to do business with. Or a restaurant or hotel who makes you feel like royalty and gets it right every time.

What could your business achieve if you created those moments for your customers ... or even something close to it?

When Reality Fails to Match Expectations

Browsing online for a Niagara Falls getaway during an extended speaking tour uncovered a well-known chain with an amazingly easy-to-use website and exactly the Falls-view room and little extras that I was looking for. It stood out above all the others.

I was blown away by their lead-up to my stay — welcoming e-mails, the opportunity to personalize my stay with some advance concierge-type offerings (a nice Ramp Up strategy selling value-add extras). It was a beautiful, deliberately-crafted "wow." On check-in there were some unexpected goodies, but also a couple of minor glitches that were easy to overlook as my first impressions were still so positive. Then, the Experience started to fall apart.

Internet was an extra. The restaurant closed unexpectedly early the night we tried to use that part of our packaged stay. They did not live up to the "green" program touted throughout the room. An error on the bill made check-out unpleasant and the valet service was chaotic. Once back in my office, I was bombarded for weeks with discount deals to stay at the hotel again. Then it all went silent.

Expectations were set at a high level. The Experience did not match up. As a result, Perceived Quality went from high to low, despite the fact that they had high Functional Quality, including a wonderful property, beautiful rooms with fantastic views, and great food, all because of the highs and lows in their Experiential Quality.

I shudder to think that staying at this chain again may open up my in-box to a similar barrage.

Your Takeaway: Look for disconnects between your company's intention and the reality you deliver.

GAP #3
Quality Equation: Perceived Quality = Functional Quality + Experiential Quality

You want to define quality much more broadly than just product specifications before you can get untethered and find straightforward practical ways to build Perceived Quality into every touch point throughout the customer Experience. Instead, many leaders continue to define quality as a product-related factor and spend more time, money, and effort there than is justified, when greater returns lie elsewhere.

Achieving the gold standard for Functional Quality in a product/service (i.e., Six Sigma) may be well beyond the financial means of your organization and may be well beyond what your customers need and are willing to pay for. Sometimes a dime-store hammer gets the job done just as well as the professional version costing many times more, and Value Creation Conversations will help you sanity check this crucial element.

However, being the gold standard in terms of how the customer *feels* when they do business with you is highly desirable and it's achievable for every company with the will to pursue that goal. "Good enough to get the job done" wrapped in a great Experience is the sweet spot for many firms, unless your industry requires exacting tolerances.

As noted earlier you can't manage a customer relationship, but you can deliberately *craft* and *manage* the Customer Experience to build a corporate Reputation for Quality that drives retention and loyalty. Customers can only have three types of experiences — good, bad, or bland. When you implement the Value Creation Conversation approach, you'll know exactly where your current experiences rank.

Grabbing the Top Spot

Who is the gold standard in your industry for the Experiences they create for their customers?

If you can't name them or it's not you, it's a sign that you are missing out on one of the most valuable opportunities to differentiate, support premium prices, and grow more quickly than the rest of your industry. Because that is exactly what a high Reputation for Quality delivers to whoever grabs the top spot on an Experiential level.

Your Takeaway: Being the gold standard for Experiential Quality triggers right-brain buy-in by your customers, and is virtually unbeatable.

Consequences
The Needless Opportunity Cost of Business as Usual

Taking action to dramatically improve your Perceived Quality might seem like a "nice to do someday" but who's got time for that? *You* do, if you have time for e-mail every day. Every time a customer has a Functional Quality problem, it triggers the logical left brain to start looking for alternatives and drives needless cost into your business to make it right. Every time a customer has an Experiential Quality problem, you damage your brand and trigger their emotional right brain to start looking at alternatives. You decrease your Perceived Quality and create bad word of mouth every time you increase their hassle factor, waste their time, or prevent them from doing what they're trying to do with your product or service in the first place. And as if that wasn't enough, you drive even more cost into your business with the number of people required to staff your customer service lines, escalation to busy managers, and doing whatever it takes to make it right. Those are huge profitability leaks that can rarely be accounted for in detail on your bottom line and over time, it gets taken for granted that it's a cost of doing business. It's not! It's a self-inflicted wound on the part of your company that needs your attention.

If you have a busy customer service group fully engaged in the break/fix side of your business, then that's the first thing to address. Not only are you losing out on straightforward opportunities to dominate your market space by building a Reputation for Quality, but you're accepting needlessly high Unnecessary-Costs-to-Serve that simply don't need to be there. Opportunities for new and repeat business based on Perceived Quality in your market space will drive your Top-Line Growth, and eliminating Unnecessary-Costs-to-Serve will drive your strong Bottom-Line Growth. Both of them are impacted by the overlooked opportunity to build a Reputation for Quality by delivering great Experiences.

Be True to Your Experience Statement

> Someone did a lot of work to carefully craft a great front-end Experience at that Niagara hotel. Others fell down on the delivery and on the follow through bombardment. I'm sure that this hotel chain's Experience Statement is not "Build them up, let them down, and pester them to death," but that's what they delivered.
>
> What's your Experience Statement? And what are you really delivering?
>
> *Your Takeaway: Don't guess. Find out in your Value Creation Conversations.*

We all know how annoying a creaky door hinge can be. A creaky Tinman in your organization sounds just as bad. I want you hearing that keeps-me-awake-all-night creak in your head until you take action. You're reading this book because you want to transform your business. All you lack is the right systematic approach to achieve that.

Solutions in Plain Sight
Create the Singing, Dancing, Creak-Free Tinman

As many firms simply don't have the time or resources to fully embrace the full Six Sigma process as a way of doing business, I'll give you practical, proven strategies, like the Quality Equation, that are straightforward and highly effective for product-focused organizations *and* service providers, yet less all-consuming to implement. It's more important to create a Perception of Quality than to chase perfection. The concepts of Six Sigma are inherent in these strategies, that is, preventing defects and errors in the Experience from happening in the first place and minimizing the waste and resources required to deliver a great Experience.

It's not enough just to oil the Tinman in terms of providing Functional Quality. You want to layer in Experiential Quality to make him sing and dance. A bland, boring Tinman in the *Wizard of Oz* would never have captured the hearts of millions the way the engaging personality that had a heart did.

 ## SOLUTION IN PLAIN SIGHT #1
Deal With Issues Once, on First Contact

When you define the *outcome* you're trying to create as "resolve on first contact," you can then help your resources make it happen.

Customers know that things will go wrong occasionally. All they really expect is for you to make it right without a lot of hassle and run-around. Most organizations treat their customers as salmon swimming upstream by putting resources with the ability to say "yes" or fix the problem as far away as possible from where the customer Experience has gone awry. And if you've ever seen salmon spawning, you know how bruised and battered those salmon look after fighting their way upstream.

Customers get exhausted from having to tell their story multiple times while their issue is repeatedly moved up the ladder without resolution. They get disappointed by the delays in making it right and often are angry because they have better things to do with their time. Is that the Quality Experience you're really trying to create? Of course not!

The potential time and cost savings are substantial. Research has repeatedly shown that front-line staff who are empowered to address customer issues completely the first time, actually give away *less* in concessions than more senior staff do after receiving an escalated issue.

Furthermore, it's estimated that the average CEO spends *over 20% of their time* somehow involved in resolving customer issues that have been escalated to his or her level. What a waste! That is *not* where the fun is in your business.

If you're like many companies, you end up resolving most of your customer service issues … eventually. Instead, make the commitment to resolve issues *on first contact*. Simply let your people on the front lines say "yes" as long as the solution is consistent with your Experience Statement that you'll develop with the Rapid Results Resources.

"Lean" Your Experience to Skyrocket Quality

A pipe manufacturing company was already familiar with Lean concepts on their shop floor. When they identified the categories of service issues that were causing 80% of their service costs through their Value Creation Conversations, they found many similar concepts applied to the Experiential side of their Quality Equation.

They put the "tools" (answers) near the "workstation" (their front-line customer service people). They examined their processes for opportunities to strip out waste everywhere and found it. They not only committed to solve on first contact, but also took a Root Cause Analysis approach to eliminate their most common service issues for good. In all but the rarest of cases, they eliminated the costs of having to return issue-related phone calls, escalate issues, follow arcane and time-consuming policy-and-procedure-based processes, or offer compensation for the customer's hardship. They saved almost one million dollars in the first year alone.

Their Reputation for Quality skyrocketed as did their bottom line once they eliminated Unnecessary-Costs-to-Serve while actually improving their service levels.

Rapid Results Resources: Find out how you can take immediate action on five factors that are causing 80% of your service costs at www.ProfitIn PlainSight.com/DeliverQuality.

SOLUTION IN PLAIN SIGHT #2

Deal With Obvious Self-Inflicted Wounds that Affect Perceived Quality With Root Cause Analysis

Take Perceived Quality to the next level. Ask yourself, "If we're going to resolve customer issues anyway and if we've made progress to resolve them on first contact, why don't we simply *get it right the first time*?"

I want you to go back to the beginning of this Challenge and really ponder on the question of how the culture of your company would change if all the time and energy that's currently going into *fixing problems* after the fact was redirected to *value-add activities*. Then ask yourself how committed you are to achieving that possibility in your company.

The most successful Lean implementations give every worker the authority to stop the line to resolve traditional Functional Quality issues *before* they can cause problems for customers. But that's not what happens in most organizations on the Experiential side. In fact, the vast majority of calls to call centers result from shortfalls on the part of your company that create an issue for the customer. Consider short shipments and backorders. Late deliveries. Poor packaging that results in damaged product. Services delivered by a junior resource who's competent, but doesn't leave the customer with a sense of confidence. People who don't return phone calls as promised. Errors in order entry that result in returns, credits, and a scramble to get the customer the right product. Invoices, refunds, or credit notes that aren't processed promptly or accurately. Those are self-inflicted wounds — every last one of them.

Most often, we tend to blame the *people* for quality problems; and most often it's the *process* that is flawed. So don't play the blame game. Instead, you want to get to the real source of the ongoing issues rather than simply solving each instance with costly Band-Aid fixes.

I recommend you have some fun with a day-long Root Cause Analysis Marathon. Get your service team in a room, divide and conquer the most pressing issues that surfaced in your Value Creation Conversations, and go right to the root of why they're happening so that you can eliminate many of these issues for good. You'll strip the unnecessary costs associated with them right out of the business, and free up your team for value-add work. Significant savings drop right to the bottom line and customers are delighted when you let them know they've been heard and you've taken action to make their lives easier. Complete details for how to conduct a Root Cause Analysis Marathon are in the Rapid Result Resources.

Keep It Simple and Straightforward

When a major computer manufacturer dug into their service woes and categorized their service issues, they found two major opportunities.

They found that 90% of calls from new buyers were related to a set-up instruction that was unclear. The solution? A simple decal added to the finished product prior to packaging.

All of those service calls were eliminated for mere pennies and they avoided the high overhead costs of having to expand their call center and hire additional staff as their sales increased.

Your Takeaway: Stop Band-Aiding. Fix it for good.

SOLUTION IN PLAIN SIGHT #3
Staple Yourself to the Entire Experience

Getting the creaks out of the Tinman is a great start. Now it's time for him to sing and dance. Expand your view from merely "fixing" issues to looking for ways to fine-tune and improve the Experiential Quality of every interaction your customers have with you. It's time to find more Lettuce!

In 2004, *Harvard Business Review* reprinted a landmark article entitled "Staple Yourself to an Order."[3] Although it's a bit dated now that the Internet has become such a factor in business, the article outlined a simple and effective approach to looking at every stage in the manufacturing process to uncover opportunities for improvement. When I work with manufacturing clients or service providers, we take an updated approach and "Staple Ourselves to the Entire Experience," from the time a customer first becomes aware of them to end-of-life recycling or disposal and everything in between.

During your Value Creation Conversations with your customers, you'll gain competitive insights when hearing from customers not only what is memorable — either good or bad — about their Experiences with *your company*, but also what they appreciate and dislike about their Experiences with your *competition*, and various *other* suppliers they deal with. Most often my clients report back

---

[3] *Benson P. Shapiro, V. Kasturi Rangan and John J. Sviokla, "Staple Yourself to an Order," in* Harvard Business Review *July-August 2004, at pages 113-121; originally published in 1992.*

that they uncover surprising and disturbing "you're too hard to do business with" feedback that they never expected.

Although that input comes as an unpleasant surprise, the good news is that once it has surfaced it can be dealt with. You can start to differentiate from the competition by creating a pleasant path-of-least-resistance approach instead. If you've ever seen the formal sidewalks on a college campus or neighborhood park, criss-crossed with informal footpaths that get people where they need to go faster, you know what I'm talking about. You know instinctively that when you try to force-fit customers onto a path that doesn't work for them, the path they'll choose instead will often be your competition.

While all aspects are important from a Quality Perspective, ensure that you don't dismiss the peace-of-mind and feel-good components that you learned about in the Find Your Lettuce component — the first of Seven Ramp Up Strategies. It applies here too. Otherwise, you'll only address the logical left side of the brain rather than the emotional right side of decision-making, and you'll miss out on a powerful way to differentiate yourself from the competition.

Complexity Versus Path of Least Resistance

One IT product and services firm who implemented the Staple Yourself to the Entire Experience process was aghast at just how much complexity and how many mixed messages and costly workarounds had crept into the Experience they offered customers over the years.

When they stripped it back to a simple, pleasant path-of-least-resistance that better matched their customers' ideal supplier profile, the first successes they found were a reduction in inventory by a factor of five and elimination of all over-time that had been required just to make the cumbersome processes work. Perceived Quality soared.

This triggered insights that helped them Find their Lettuce. They layered in new ways to save the client time, save them money, solve a real problem, create peace of mind, or make them feel good ... and returned to profitability for the first time in 5 years.

Your Takeaway: Are you the path of least resistance, or an obstacle course?

Use the Comprehensive Resources — Never Reinvent the Wheel

Conceptually, creating a Corporate Reputation for Quality is easy when we really understand what level of quality a customer is looking for and then flawlessly deliver the solutions they need. The challenge is finding the sweet spot for both Functional and Experiential Quality to create a high level of Perceived Quality. Leaders and managers tell me that they've never really connected with their customers to find out if the dime-store hammer or a more expensive option is really required — they assume that they have to provide the highest level of Functional Quality. Often they know that they have a busy customer service department, yet have never stepped back to ask why that is the case and how it could be different. Most neglect the Experiential side simply because they've never been taught why it's so critical to right-brain decision-making and how to move beyond conventional quality aspects to create it.

The systematic Profit in Plain Sight Framework is unique in that it uses the information in the Value Creation Conversations to capture *top-of-mind* quality issues, rather than trying to identify *every* issue, enabling you to prioritize what to address first. The Framework then provides practical, proven tactics that deliver results. When you're ready to transform your Perceived Quality and become the gold standard for your industry rather than settling for business as usual, you don't have to reinvent any wheels, you just need to implement the Profit and Growth Accelerators embedded in the Framework, and available to you in the Rapid Results Resources.

Summary

Prevention is worth a pound of cure. Even when product and service issues are resolved, they harm your company's Reputation for Quality. They cost your customers time and inconvenience that can make them susceptible to grass-is-greener competitive offers, costing you market share, volume and profits, and damaging your reputation. They are a huge hidden cost within your business that hurts your bottom line, not only because of the actual costs to make it right, but because of the time and energy wasted to repeatedly fix what's gone wrong rather than move the organization forward. And they hinder your ability to scale for growth or even to grow at all if they result in negative word of mouth.

This isn't a "nice to do someday." You want to take action on this immediately, even if you've already invested in having great Functional Quality. The rewards of achieving a Reputation for Quality and becoming the gold standard in your business will transform your business and the relationships you have with your customers, just as the rusted Tinman transformed into Dorothy's trusted ally. Rusted or trusted? Your choice!

As with all things in business, developing and maintaining a corporate Reputation for Quality is an ongoing process. Just as exposure to the elements caused the Tinman in the *Wizard of Oz* to seize up, every organization degrades over time and eventually quality becomes an issue without a concerted effort to keep it well oiled. When organizational corrosion takes hold, both the work environment *and* competitive advantage are destroyed.

You can spend a lot of time to determine how to improve Perceived Quality on your own or you can use proven approaches that deliver results.

You've learned how to activate the Quality Equation by addressing every aspect of the Experiential Quality your customers receive every time they interact with your company. You've seen straightforward steps to minimize waste — of time, resources, energy, attention, rework (not just on products), and lapses in quality that are very visible to clients and staff. When you deal with Experiential Quality issues at a root cause level, you'll drive out self-inflicted service costs and put more on your bottom line.

Act on the three Solutions in Plain Sight and you'll quickly and easily develop a corporate Reputation for Quality as a company that gets it right the first time that will be hard for your competitors to emulate or beat.

This Works. You Can Do It. You Will Succeed.

Take these Actions

Transformation takes more than awareness and good intentions.

Assessment	1. Take 11 minutes to complete the "Profit in Plain Sight Assessment" at *www.ProfitInPlainSight.com/Profit* and pass the link along to your team so that you can compare notes.
Resource	2. Take immediate action in less time than you're currently spending on e-mail when you access Rapid Results Resources to eliminate five factors that are causing 80 percent of your service costs at *www.ProfitInPlainSight.com/DeliverQuality*.
Action Item	3. Schedule a team meeting to: • Ask the Tough Love questions from the beginning of this Chapter. • Hold each other accountable when you hear tethered language or observe left-brain-dominated thinking regarding quality. • Review your "Profit in Plain Sight Assessment" results and compare notes. • Evaluate what would have to change in your organization in order to enable those on the front lines to say "yes" to any reasonable solution that would resolve issues on first contact. Is your organization brave enough to give it a try? • Bring your attention to the interactions you have as a customer in your business and personal life. Which Experiences are bad, bland or good? What can you learn from them?

- Commit to stop guessing what it will take to be the gold standard in your industry. Implement Value Creation Conversations and find out.

Small Steps. Big Impact!

Five Minutes, Five Questions: Reflect for Deeper Learning

Your first step is *internal* transformation, to identify what attitudes have already shifted and what behaviors will follow.

1. How have my Perceptions of conventional Quality standards and our efforts to date to deliver Quality changed as I consider the Experiences I have with suppliers in my business and personal life?

2. How large is the gap between the gold standard in our industry and the way our customers perceive our total Quality (Experiential and Functional)? Are we needlessly too high, too low, or just right on one or the other or both?

3. What is the worst-case scenario of uncovering service issues during our Value Creation Conversations? What is the best case?

4. What positive impacts do I anticipate on our culture if we use an approach that solves many of our persistent challenges for good? What resistance do I anticipate?

5. What commitment am I willing to make to differentiate our firm from our competition by deliberately crafting an Experience that becomes the gold standard for our industry?

Inform. Inspire. Motivate. Transform.
Infuse. Enthuse.

Stimulating Innovation and Creativity and Enabling Entrepreneurship

21 Paths to Innovation that Your Competition Can't Just Copy

Creating a company that can capitalize on growth opportunities is wiser than looking for a growth industry.

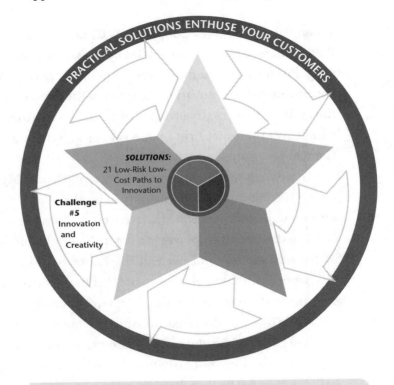

PRACTICAL SOLUTIONS ENTHUSE YOUR CUSTOMERS

SOLUTIONS:
21 Low-Risk Low-Cost Paths to Innovation

Challenge #5
Innovation and Creativity

How good would it feel if you never found yourself saying "we should have thought of that" or weren't playing catch up to your competition again because you've turned the tables — and that's what they're saying?

What would it mean to your business if you no longer had to play the discount game because your customers finally see a difference between you and all the commodity players in your marketplace — and they only want to do business with *you*?

What would be possible for your company if you were able to innovate quickly, in low-risk, low-cost ways that your competitors likely won't spot and can't copy?

When PricewaterhouseCoopers (PWC) decided to go beyond its R&D centers to find its next $100M business, the results were stunning. But how do you find ways for employees to come up with entrepreneurial, innovative ideas when they spend their days in the relatively uncreative worlds of audit, accounting, and tax in a huge international firm of 766 offices and 32,000 employees? Games. Yes, games!

An *Apprentice*-like contest called Powerpitch offered the winning team $100,000 and the opportunity to implement their idea. Over a 9-month period, over 800 ideas were created, evaluated, critiqued, and voted on by all employees to create 25 semifinalists who were paired with advisors and given billable hours to work on their plans. Five were eventually selected to present to the firm's most senior executives while the rest of the company watched via webcast.

While one was declared the official winner, PWC decided to invest in all five of the ideas and bonused each team, and the remaining 20 finalists were not forgotten, but rather assigned to an incubation group for further development.

You don't have to hold contests. You just need to learn how to stimulate creativity rather than shutting it down, how to direct the creativity to value-add *innovation* as opposed to merely creative *inventions*, and how to get good ideas off the drawing board and implemented for impact.

Low-risk, low-cost innovation that is high value-add holds the key and, contrary to popular belief, there *is* a process to stimulate it and unlock the creativity your organization has been missing.

Innovation, Creativity and Entrepreneurship Are for You When ...

... you're tired of playing catch up to your competitors;

... you're tired of having your competitors copy your good ideas in a never-ending, "new and improved" race that adds costs to your business, but no profit; and

... you know you want to add more value to your customers, but hit-and-miss innovation efforts are off-target or simply not delivering consistent breakthroughs.

Growth and profitability only come from creating value in ways that are different and better than your competitors. Breakthroughs and overnight successes rarely happen by accident. So if you find you're too often playing catch-up or falling prey to follow-the-leader strategies, you'll learn practical, proven strategies to stimulate innovation, creativity, and entrepreneurship in uncommon ways within your company.

Tough Love: Ask Your Leadership Team Five Critical Questions

1. When was the last time we did something innovative and unexpected that made our customers sit up and take notice and our competitors say "we should have thought of that?"

2. When was the last time we did something that had huge value-add for our customers but was so far below the radar screen that our competitors couldn't figure out what was going on?

3. When was the last time that our customers were willing to pay a premium to us because we're different and better than our competition?

4. What could we achieve if our high-potential employees spent as much time on value-add innovation as they do on e-mail?

5. How often are we inspired by a success story in the business press, but that story is always about someone else and we don't know how to get there?

 Rapid Results Resources: Need to jump-start Innovation and Creativity among your team? Access success stories, thought-provoking examples, and more at www.ProfitInPlainSight.com/InnovateNow.

Now, keep untethering as we debunk the myths surrounding Innovation and Creativity.

 ## Move Beyond the Myths

Which of these three myths are camouflaging your low-cost, low-risk opportunities for innovation?

FACT: There are two kinds of value that customers pay for — Functional Value that is inherent in the product and Emotional Value (which are similar to Functional and Experiential Quality, but subtly different) within the experience of doing business with you. Most companies follow an ever-increasing spiral of Functional innovation (think new and improved/bells and whistles), yet adding Emotional Value (for example, peace of mind) consistently offers higher payoffs. Once you get very clear on the concept and have a process to identify and commercialize these types of opportunities, it's relatively easy and inexpensive to achieve low-cost, low-risk innovation and, most important, it's *very* hard for your competitors to copy.

FACT: Many of the best process- and customer-value innovations *don't* come from R&D or a lab. Often those sources produce inventions but not necessarily innovation that adds value. Instead, innovations come from casting a critical eye on what the real problem is that needs to be solved and then solving it. We all think of Apple as a highly innovative company, yet as a percentage of revenue, the company spends *less than half* of what the typical computer and electronics company does and only a fifth of what Microsoft does on R&D. Instead, they focus on creating products that are a joy to use (Emotional Value) and provide a seamless experience (Experiential Quality).

The Blackberry was an innovative invention that dominated the *functional* space with its highly secure e-mail capabilities, and two-thumbs typing, prized by IT departments, left-brain thinkers, and those who spend a lot of time on e-mail and needed that functionality. In contrast, the iPhone owns the Emotional Value space. Nobody will ever say it's the best tool for e-mail, but most will agree that it's an invaluable part of their life. Android phones are largely me-to, and multiple providers yet to date have no strong positioning in their prospects' minds. "Cheaper than an iPhone" is most often given as the reason for purchase, and that's not a sustainable competitive advantage.

MYTH #2
Hit-It-Out-of-the-Ballpark Innovation Is the Best Source of Competitive Advantage

FACT: Smaller, fly-under-the-radar innovations are typically lower cost, lower risk, and more sustainable from a competitive perspective. Focus on doing 100 small things better over time — not all at once — to get a lot of base hits that put more points on the scoreboard in every inning. You'll know what some of those 100 things are as a result of your Value Creation Conversations. When you act on them, your customers may not know exactly what's different about your firm — only that they prefer to do business with you. Unlike product feature improvements, this type of innovation is hard for competitors to even spot, let alone duplicate and it may well become a hit-it-out-of-the-ballpark win. True entrepreneurs know the value of ready-*fire*-aim approaches that try a lot of things cheaply and quickly. Find out what works and what doesn't, discard ideas that are less successful, and then pursue those with promise.

MYTH #3
Incentive and Compensation Programs Have to Be Developed and Implemented to Motivate Employees' Creativity and Entrepreneurship

FACT: On the contrary, most organizations unwittingly suppress new ideas when their good intentions to encourage and reward employee contributions become unwieldy incentive programs that often simply *increase* complexity and *reduce* entrepreneurial spirit.

By the time the idea is evaluated and valued for compensation pur- poses (typically by a committee), the window of opportunity has often closed. Compensating an *individual* for an idea when a *team* of resources is required to implement it undervalues their contri- butions and often creates unrest and competition rather than col- laboration. Get the good ideas first and stay flexible to appropriately rewarding the team or individual later, bearing in mind that often the best rewards are intangibles such as autonomy, a sense of purpose, and a feeling of mastery.[1]

Expand Your Thinking to Close the Gaps
Creative Opportunities to Innovate Are
Everywhere If You Know How to Spot
Value Gaps

Innovation is more about *solutions* than raw creativity. There are books on innovation filled with stories of highly creative market failures — those were *inventions*, not *innovations*. Instead, it's about finding creative *solutions* to the problems your current and poten- tial customers are experiencing. How do you spot those problems? By listening carefully to their answers during your Value Creation Conversations or by watching them use your product.

Get out of R&D thinking and dive into Value Gaps — gaps that customers may or may not be able to articulate or gaps that you see as they fumble through work-arounds with your product that they currently take for granted and wouldn't even think to articulate. Look for gaps in Functionality and gaps in Emotional Value, such as confusion, frustration, and annoyance.

Innovation can be hard to envision, but we all know it when we see it.

---

[1] *For further discussion on the value of autonomy, a sense of purpose, and a feeling of mastery, please see Daniel H. Pink's excellent book,* Drive: The Surprising Truth About What Motivates Us *(New York: Riverhead (Penguin Group (USA)), 2009).*

Your customers can't see beyond their current concept of the product, so what they ask for is faster-better-cheaper rather than something truly innovative. As Henry Ford said, his potential customers would have simply asked for a faster horse that ate less! So don't waste your time asking what they want. The secret lies in actually seeing or understanding what they're trying to *do* and using *your* knowledge of your processes and possibilities to help them do it *better*.

Often we try to go about innovation the hard way, trying to dream up new ideas, when in fact the clues lie right in front of us. Once you understand your customers' issues and challenges, you can translate that knowledge into ways to save your customers time, save them money, solve a real problem they're grappling with, or just make them feel good. Those "we should have thought of that!" moments are in direct response to realizing that the new product or service is an obvious answer to a challenge that we hadn't spotted.

One of the biggest challenges as leaders and managers try to wrap their heads around this is that it seems too simple. Many of us learned that we're supposed to be the experts and that it's our responsibility to dream up the next big thing. On the contrary, every great product is all about helping the customer simply do what they're trying to do.

Customers Can Identify Challenges, But Not Products

Back in the days of the Sony Walkman (an innovative product in its own right), could you have envisioned and asked for an iPod and accompanying iTunes, had Sony asked what you'd wanted? Probably not.

But had Sony Stapled Itself to the Experience of a Walkman user, they would have seen them grappling with having to carry a variety of cassettes around and make up their own music mixes from other media (LPs, 8-Tracks, cassettes) to play on their Walkman. They missed a very obvious clue to the next big thing by not seeing the challenges their customers were grappling with.

Unfortunately, market research shows that customers often fail to buy what they've asked for ... but they *do* buy something that fills their want or need.

Your Takeaway: Stop asking what they want. Observe what they need.

GAP #2

The Challenge Is to Figure Out How to Make Innovation Happen by Igniting Creativity in the People Who Work With Us

Unfortunately, "Think outside the box, people!" is rarely an effective technique unless people are guided on exactly how to think that way. A student of mine in the Creative Marketing Strategies course in the University of British Columbia MBA program found it counterintuitive that *structure* actually holds the key to creative thinking. Throughout the semester he wrestled with and pushed back on the idea of structured creativity (a great sign of an active, learning mind). Finally he experienced how effectively some new frameworks and uncommon ways to structure his thinking worked with the real-world project his team had selected. He finally grasped that *structured* creative thinking that puts many new lenses on the same picture was more effective than purely attempting to be a creative "photographer" with the equivalent of a point-and-shoot camera that offered no options.

Your Value Creation Conversations provide you with a rich source of innovative ideas just waiting to be brought to life and add value. Without a structure, you'll flail around with too many unconnected ideas. However, when you can spot trends and similarities, the AHA! Moments emerge.

Yes, we've all heard that Steve Jobs never sought customer input — the reason for that is that as a frustrated-but-visionary consumer of the technology products he and others produced, he already had all the "customer insights" he needed. Unless you personally use your own products or services and are highly visionary and creative, you cannot duplicate the magic that Jobs brought to innovation.

Ban the Suggestion Box!

Have you ever made the mistake of implementing a Suggestion Box?

In most cases they start off crammed with all kinds of weird and wonderful ideas that have to end up on someone's To-Do List because you asked for them. Few if any every get implemented. Over time input dwindles to nothing or to tongue-in-cheek or ridiculous ideas.

Innovation is the same way. You don't want a flood of ideas that will bring your organization to a grinding halt. Instead, you want a systematic and effective approach to spot opportunities and develop them quickly and easily, so that your team sees the results of their efforts and is eager to contribute again. When you synthesize the input from your Value Creation Conversations and wash them through the innovation filters outlined on the following pages, you'll have the systematic approach to low-risk, low-cost innovation that you've been missing.

GAP #3

Innovation, Creativity and Entrepreneurship Have Been Beaten Out of Most of Us

It's hard to recapture our entrepreneurial spirit without the right support structure. A child learning to walk and adults providing encouragement and support is the perfect metaphor for entrepreneurial spirit — the child is compelled to pull him- or herself up and figure out how to get where it wants to go, even with stumbles along the way. The child is not shy to reach out for help and knows that those helping hands will be there.

Imagine if we expected a newborn to have figured out how to walk perfectly. Or if we did the equivalent of chaining them to a desk with no opportunity to explore for themselves, to try new things, to improve, or to finally stand up and take their first step.

Innovative companies allow time for play and for experimentation. Most companies ask their employees to keep their heads down and get the job done. Who are we fooling?

Sowing the Seeds of Innovation and Creativity

Unfortunately, by about 5 years old a child starts learning that "mistakes are bad" and that "failure is punished," and over the rest of his or her life will repeatedly hear "that will never work," "what a dumb idea," "that was a waste of time," and "who do you think you are?" Where did those supportive, encouraging, helping hands go?

No wonder our employees don't have a lot of creativity or

innovative entrepreneurial spirit left by the time they reach their career years!

However, when you implement the Return on People metric from Possibility Driver #1 in a way that's supportive and encouraging, you've already sown the seeds for entrepreneurship and innovation. When you engage your organization in creating your Customer Profitability Diamond to change their mind-set about profitability, involve them in implementing the 5Rs for Proactively Managing Customer Profitability, challenge them to undertake Root Cause Analysis, and have them Staple Themselves to the Entire Experience, you sow new seeds of creativity. All you need to do is fertilize those seeds with focus and provide guidance with helping hands. Your people, properly supported, will feel compelled to figure out how to create an Innovation and Creativity harvest.

Your Takeaway: Sow the seeds with helping hands.

Consequences
You Risk Becoming Road Kill With Business as Usual

"Innovate or Die" screams one headline. "Run Like the Rest and You Too Will be Road Kill" says another. One thing they have in common is that selling your current products and services to your current customers is a sure-fire approach to stagnation and death as you get run over by new ideas in your market space. Yet the process of innovation is simply not a consistent mainstream business practice for most companies. You're losing opportunities every day to drive Passion, Profit, and Growth in your business.

Taking action on Innovation and Creativity might seem like a "nice to do," but who's got time for that? *You* do. You can't justify spending more time on e-mail than you do on Innovation and Creativity. When your competitors enter the market with the usual new-and-improved approach, you get left behind the eight ball, drive cost into your business as you struggle to catch up, lose customers to something better, and get stuck using price to woo them back to your "me too" solution. You have competitors in the global economy who aren't even on your radar yet — companies that don't even exist other than in someone's mind or garage but are developing solutions for the problems your customers have that you're not even seeing. Conventional product enhancements that can be copied in China in a week at lower prices aren't the answer, it's the problem. You want new ways to create and deliver value-add solutions to your customers so that you can grow instead of shrink. You can't afford to get the kind of transformational wake-up call that has put so many good companies out of business, especially if you have the same sort of surprises lurking in your business … and you probably do.

If You Don't Innovate, Someone Else Will Eat Your Lunch

Think about the airline hot-meal providers who saw their business vanish overnight when the airlines eliminated that service to cut costs. Now, you may not think of the airline-food business as highly innovative, but think again.

Companies that were not traditional competitors to the established hot-food suppliers saw an explosion of new opportunities to create new products, because the airlines' customers' hunger pangs didn't simply go away just because meal service was discontinued! They treated the airlines as potential new customers and offered them new solutions. Hot meals were replaced with snack packages, soup mixes, sandwiches, wraps, and more. That business likely could have gone to the existing food suppliers, had they been innovative and acted quickly instead of trying to fight the tidal wave of reality.

A new supply chain appeared. Airport restaurants who would never have been on the hot-food suppliers' competitive radar screens suddenly sold far beyond their traditional floor-space and capitalized on the disruption in the market with value-add buy-to-go services that cut the airlines out altogether and yet are consumed on the *outbound* side of the boarding gate. If Innovation and Creativity in their most basic definitions can happen in the mundane food-for-airline-consumption industry, it can happen in your industry too.

Nobody was in a better position to know that there was a real problem to be solved than the hot-food suppliers. Nobody missed the boat as badly as they did by trying to do business as usual.

Your Takeaway: Innovation does not have to be big and flashy. It just needs to solve a real problem.

You can't stay where you are and survive. You can't pursue conventional approaches and thrive. You want to find a better alternative. Every time you look at the tray table in front of you when you're traveling by air, I want you to be just a little bit paranoid about who's about to eat your lunch. And I want you to take action on Innovation and Creativity. All you lack is the right systematic approach to transform your business and the competitive landscape.

Solutions in Plain Sight
Low-Risk, Low-Cost Innovation Is Hidden
in Your Business

If you're seeing change in your industry, you can either hunker down and try to stave off the inevitable with business as usual or you can use it to spur innovation.

Maturing markets, commoditization, and foreign-made knock-offs are emerging challenges for almost every business, but whenever markets mature, emerging markets appear. Whenever one part of the value chain is suffering from commoditization, decommoditization is at work in another — at different stages, in different layers of value.

Increasingly, off-the-radar substitutes and entirely new business models blindside companies who fail to scan the environment broadly enough for innovative opportunities.

The challenge is to use a set of disciplined innovation filters to challenge "we've always done it this way" thinking and spot opportunities for value creation across the many insights that will surface from your Value Creation Conversations. The big secret to creativity and entrepreneurship is in helping employees actively engage in a structured process of questioning, observing, and experimenting to develop not only the next big idea, but the next small one that helps you differentiate and add value at every stage.

When you filter what you've heard in your Value Creation Conversations through the 21 Low-Risk, Low-Cost Paths to Innovation, your path to innovation will become very clear. All of these are illustrated in Figure 1.

Figure 1: 21 LOW-RISK, LOW-COST PATHS TO INNOVATION

The Product Life Cycle (Figure 2)	The Innovation Cocktail Framework (Figure 5)
1. Product Innovation	14. Low-Churn/Low-Growth Sweet Spot in Existing Products/Markets
2. Application Innovation	
3. Process Innovation	15. Warm and Fuzzy Enhancements
4. Experiential Innovation	
5. Marketing Innovation	16. Promoter Status in New Products or Services
6. Business Model Innovation	
7. Reverse Positioning	17. Image Building Pioneer during Expansion
8. Stealth Positioning	
9. Breakaway Positioning	18. Kiss of Life Repositioning
10. Scratch an Itch Innovation	19. Organic Growth and Retention Positioning
11. Underserved Innovation	
12. Bust Bottlenecks	20. New Customer Converts
13. Adjacency Innovation	21. Enviable Breakthrough Success

SOLUTION IN PLAIN SIGHT #1

13 Paths to Innovation Are Hidden in Your Classic Product Life Cycle

You may have learned about the conventional Product Life Cycle in a long-ago marketing class, but this fresh approach is guaranteed to strike creative sparks and generate growth opportunities. Innovation is rarely an issue during the run-up to product maturity, as growing markets and new-and-improved options often provide more than enough growth for a company to cope with, so we'll focus on finding new opportunities in mature markets.

I'm going to assume that your business operates in a mature market, providing goods and services that genuinely solve customer problems, rather than speaking to readers who are focused on the start-up and disruptive stages. However, when you look at the success of the "we have an app for that" industry that's sprung up around smart phones, you will find that many successful start-ups have simply focused on the classic approach of saving you time, saving you money, solving a real problem, creating peace of mind, or offering a feel-good. And that is why people now spend more time in the app world than they spend on the web, which used to be the go-to resource.

Spend less and innovate more when you leverage the Product Life Cycle for growth.

Sustained and steady growth is all about having a framework to help you explore opportunities to generate profitable business throughout *every* stage of the Product Life Cycle, based on the intersection of what problems a customer needs solved and what you're good at or could be good at (see Figure 2).

Figure 2: LEVERAGE THE PRODUCT LIFE CYCLE FOR GROWTH

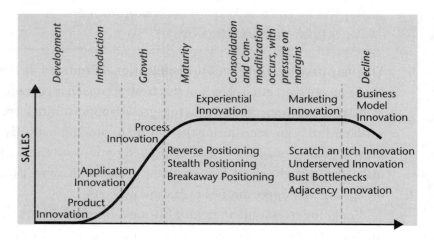

 Rapid Results Resources: As it would take more pages than there are in this entire book to do justice to explaining the how-to's for each of these opportunities I've put them all together in the Innovation in Plain Sight Resources that you can access at www.ProfitInPlain Sight.com/InnovateNow. You'll be able to evaluate ideas in your own business with that tool. However, in the meantime I want to shed some additional light on the big picture and get you stirred up.

It's well known that Apple is considered one of of the most innovative companies in the world. Their secrets to success become apparent when you see how well they have leveraged each and every Innovation in Plain Sight opportunity in the Product Life Cycle in Figure 2. The table in Figure 3 gives you a bird's-eye view of how they did it.

The big challenge many leaders grapple with is that having the structure for idea generation is *not enough*; it's staying out of overwhelm territory. When you develop only the most promising ideas and are willing to ready-*fire*-aim, that's a good start for keeping things manageable. The other way to stay away from feeling overwhelmed and keeping the momentum going after the initial rush is to create a *process* for ongoing ideation and implementation, rather than settling for a sporadic event-type approach. The Innovation in Plain Sight Resources will not only give you all the structured creative frameworks and processes you need to delve more deeply into insights you gathered in your Value Creation Conversations, but they will also help you stay empowered rather than overpowered.

The research on Innovation and Creativity keeps coming back to just two things — develop a deep and ongoing understanding of your customer and a deep understanding of your core strengths. Then, leverage both to create new value in new ways.

As you interpret what you've heard in your Value Creation Conversations, ask yourselves "What job are they hiring our product to do?" Nobody wants to buy the drill; what they *really* want is the hole it makes. When you find out what they're trying to do and find better ways to help them do it, that's true value-add innovation you'll be able to take to the bank. On the other hand, cool inventions that don't address a real need, like the infamous Segway, may offer technological innovation but if they don't add value, they will not be commercially successful.

Figure 3: APPLE AND THE PRODUCT LIFE CYCLE

	Introduction — Attracts interest and early adopters	Growth — Gain acceptance, loyalty, and mass-market appeal	Maturity — Consolidation and Commoditization occurs	Decline — Customers want relief from Market Dominators and are ready for something new
1. Product Innovation: New and Improved	Apple II Macintosh	Multiple desktop models Cube	iMac all-in-one	
2. Application Innovation: New markets, unexploited uses	Desktop publishing	Home Education	iPod Touch (includes games such as Angry Birds)	
3. Process Innovation: Addresses "plug and play" needs	Apple TV	Powerbook — first built-in mouse (trackball)		Windows software can be installed on Macs – expanding the range of Mac users
4. Stealth Positioning: Eliminate sresistance to an unpopular or failed concept	iPads start to convert hard-core PC users, unlike previous tablets			
5. Reverse Positioning: Simplifies or adds surprising new features	Graphical interface iPod	Bright colours	iPod Nano MacBook Air	iBooks2 starts to replace the outdated textbook model
6. Breakaway Positioning: Combines features of products in distinctly different categories	iPhone	iPhone 3G, 3GS iPad 2	iPhone 4, 4GS	

Type of Innovation			
7. Experiential Innovation: Enhances every interaction	iPods change the MP3 experience iPhones change the smart phone experience forever		White earbuds replace boring black ones and help "brand" Apple customers
8. Marketing Innovation: Out-sells rather than out-product		Apple Stores	Environmentally friendly glass and aluminum unibody cases, not plastic
9. Business Model Innovation: reframes the value chain			Apple Store changes the face of retail electronics
10. Scratch an Itch Innovation: Plays to frustration, makes it easy	Apps for everything	Integrated speakers Color screen	
11. Underserved Innovation: Prospers at the low end		Apple supported Mac clones in the 1990s	iPod shuffle
12. Bust Bottlenecks: Democratizes, removes barriers to consumption (i.e., skills, access, wealth)	iTunes for music iCloud for document sharing		
13. Adjacency Innovation: Moves existing clients to related-but-different products and services		iPad & iPhone users quickly adopt and adapt to iPads	

Gutsy Decision, Whole-Brain Thinking, and Innovation

When a car dealership looked at their opportunities to innovate, they decided to innovate on the marketing side of their business as there was little they could do on the product side. They decided to offer free fuel for a year rather than discount their vehicles to match the competition.

Not a speck of R&D dollars were required for that Marketing Innovation, but it gave them something different to talk about in their crowded, mature market space and, most importantly, provided a value-add to customers that went way beyond offering free floor mats or undercoating. That simple Marketing Innovation created a tremendous buzz that brought in new customers in the way that a "match-the-price" discount never would. It gave customers the confidence to enter the dealership knowing that the usual discounting games wouldn't be played and created a feel-good to the purchase process. Unlike a quickly-forgotten discount, the dealer reinforced their buying decision as a positive experience every time their customer fueled up.

Yes, technically a competitor could copy that move, but they didn't because they hadn't taken the time to figure out how to manage the risk. Once the dealer owned that high ground others would clearly be seen simply as copycats.

It wasn't easy to make the gutsy decision to implement such a bold move, but it was straightforward, low risk, and low cost once the dealer used whole-brain thinking. They had to evaluate the risk — what if the fuel cost more than the discount? They looked to the data they had on what kind of mileage customers did between servicing and figured it out. Surprisingly, it cost the dealer less to give away the fuel than what he would have discounted on the initial vehicle purchase. When the various volume bonuses he earned from the manufacturer by moving more cars were factored in along with reduced cost of inventory by getting greater turns, the dealership came out significantly to the good.

Your Takeaway: Use the Product Life Cycle filters to find the hot buttons others have overlooked.

SOLUTION IN PLAIN SIGHT #2
Unleash Your Innovation Cocktail

Mixology has become a big trend these days. That in and of itself is an innovation in the restaurant business that has delivered bottom-line results well beyond the typical margins of beer and wine. But the point is that if you look at award-winning cocktails, they usually demonstrate an optimal blend of two elements: sweet and sour, color and flavor, alcohol and mix, and so on. For this stage of low-cost, low-risk innovation, I want you to think of the optimal blend of Functional Value *and* Emotional Value (which are similar to Functional and Experiential Quality, but subtly different). We've come full circle back to right-brain and left-brain thinking.

Buying decisions are almost always driven first by Emotional Value long before a customer has any experiences with the product, then justified by Functional Value, and lastly justified by price. Most of us were taught to create and sell products and services based on *features and benefits* and to default to price when necessary to close the deal — a completely backwards approach as it focuses purely on Functional Value.

The Innovation Cocktail Framework is X parts Functional Value + Y parts Emotional Value and that recipe provides the eight additional opportunities for successful innovation listed in the 21 Low-Risk, Low-Cost Paths to Innovation (see Figure 1). It also identifies eight common approaches to Innovation and Creativity that will fail. When leaders and their teams learn to systematically explore each of the eight overlooked opportunities to increase value not just with product enhancements, but by adding stealthy Emotional Value, they create innovations that are almost impossible for competitors to identify, let alone copy. You'll see these shortly.

How often do you see a Request for Proposal (RFP) full of functional specs and deliverables? Among those who meet the functional requirements, don't we assume that the final decision usually relies heavily on price? More often the final decision relies on some intangible *emotional* benefit that the customer has registered in their right brain. Having been on both sides of the sealed-bid process, I can attest to the unmistakable fact that previously determined *emotional* choices are frequently simply justified by the bid process.

Emotional Value Trumped Features and Price

One vendor who effectively broke out of the functional and pricing traps years ago was IBM and they continue to own the right-brain Emotional Value in their customers' minds today, even though they have completely changed their business model.

You may remember the days when computers were still big, bulky, and relatively new. The water-cooler conversations in the IT Department often revolved around "nobody ever got fired for buying IBM" when new acquisitions were being contemplated. While IBM didn't always have the best products compared to their competitors, they overcame buyers' perception of computer investments as a high risk by creating an impeccable perception that IBM was the low-risk option.

IBM equipment provided good Functional Value and, more importantly, career safety and peace of mind as a decision that nobody could ever question or criticize. IBM owned the low-risk space in their customers' minds as a result of carefully crafting a safe, business-like image with the classic navy blue suit and white shirt. Every other supplier had to be significantly better on price and functionality just to be on the playing field — and IBM still was most often the winner.

Buyers would often subconsciously or consciously write a Request for Proposal (RFP) that favored IBM, because *in their minds, the buying decision had already been made* — they just needed to justify it. When IBM thus scored as the "most compliant" bidder to the tailored RFP, lower priced vendors were automatically eliminated. Even in the case of multiple compliant bidders with similar prices, the decision was often better safe than sorry — IBM rather than another.

Your Takeaway: Innovations in Emotional Value can make you the vendor of choice. Period.

What would it mean to your business to have RFPs written with you and only you in mind? It's all about adequate Functional Value and extraordinary Emotional Value.

The Conventional Approach to Innovation Offers Just Four Opportunities

Let's review the conventional approach for a moment (see Figure 4), just so you'll be clear about what's different with the Innovation Cocktail Framework. You already have several effective strategies to capitalize on the conventional innovation framework as an outcome of your Value Creation Conversations.

If you want authentic loyalty and repurchase behavior to soar, then move all of your products and services to the functional/emotional sweet spots using the Innovation Cocktail Framework (Figure 5), which layers in the eight opportunities for Emotional Value.

Figure 4: THE CONVENTIONAL INNOVATION FRAMEWORK

	Existing **CUSTOMERS** New	
New	**B.** **New and Improved Products or Business Models** Offering new or improved products and services to existing customers is an advanced version of the classic Ramp Up approach. When your Innovations result from either the Product Life Cycle or the Innovation Cocktail Framework, it's almost impossible for competitors to copy. In contrast, bells and whistles, which don't reflect deep customer knowledge, are likely to be duplicated by your competitors, and at lower prices.	**A.** **Breakthrough Ideas, Technologies, or Market Insights** We all recognize breakthrough Innovation when we see it and it's often the result of long-term, costly R&D efforts beyond the reach of many companies. However, not all breakthroughs have to follow that approach when lower risk, lower cost, easier-to-spot opportunities abound in this quadrant as illustrated in the Innovation Cocktail Framework below (Figure 5).
Existing	**D.** **Eventual Stagnation Today's Products Sold to Today's Customers** Stagnation eventually occurs if you simply continue to offer existing products and services to existing customers. Right now, that's what you have to work with to generate profit and growth. That's why it's so important to Retain your most profitable customers, Regain lost customers, Ramp Up marginally profitable customers, Reactivate dormant customers, and Restore profits from unprofitable customers – the 5Rs for Proactively Managing Customer Profitability. First, maximize your opportunities in this quadrant, then use your Value Creation Conversations to identify how to move beyond it.	**C.** **Geographic Expansion or Product Positioning** Expanding geographically to source new customers or finding new uses for existing products can be effective when you identify your Ideal Customers with an advanced strategy in the Profit in Plain Sight Framework and then use that knowledge to enter new markets. If you simply enter new markets with Functional Value, you'll likely find yourself in a destructive price war, where the incumbent has the advantage.

(Left vertical axis label: **PRODUCTS AND SERVICES**)

NOTE: The darker the shading, the higher the value.

Figure 5: INNOVATION COCKTAIL FRAMEWORK

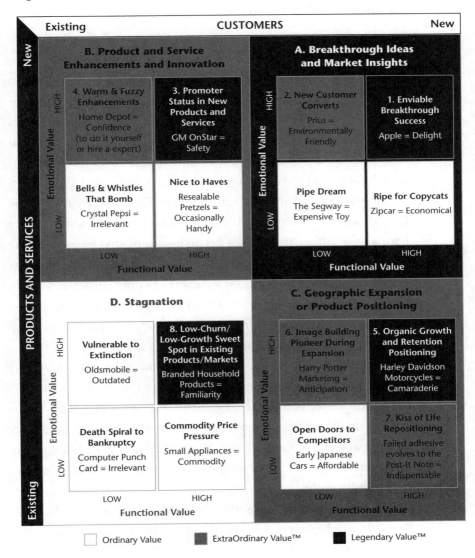

Eight Innovation-in-Plain-Sight Sweet Spots that Your Competitors Can't Copy

The power of the Innovation Cocktail Framework is unknown to most organizations. When Functional Value is overlaid with Emotional Value, you have clear innovation winners. The diagram in Figure 5 illustrates the eight sweet spots in any company's innovation framework, with examples. You'll note that the conventional matrix has simply been overlaid with a new functional/emotional lens. The darker the shading, the higher the Emotional and Functional Value and the more successful the Innovation Cocktail.

Do you notice the difference between Emotional Value terms like "delight," "safety," and "camaraderie" versus "occasionally handy?" or "affordable"? *Handy* can be duplicated by any similar product — there is no strong emotional bond. It doesn't mean that the product won't be successful, just that competitors can easily intrude on that market space. *Delight* is a powerful emotion that is difficult to recreate and impossible for your competitors to copy once you own that space in the customer's mind.

For now, think about the last three products you've launched and map them to the relevant grid of the Innovation Cocktail Framework. Are you in the stagnation stage or overly focused on Functional Value that competitors can copy? Have you made it to Emotional Value or Enviable Breakthrough Success? These diagrams illustrate that you may be losing out on many, many low-risk, low-cost opportunities.

Every Solution in Plain Sight prior to this has given you the tools to create a rich source of inspiration to fill in the sweet spots in the Cocktail Framework. This builds on the insights that you've gathered during your Value Creation Conversations. It also draws from your Staple Yourself to the Entire Experience thinking.

I Practice What I Preach

Consulting is a very mature industry, yet technology has opened up new opportunities to add value in innovative ways and shift from a local business model to one that includes mentoring, coaching, and supporting clients around the world.

Many business leaders welcome a "learn-by-doing" approach that engages their teams and creates a learning organization unlike traditional consulting and without time away from the office for seminars and training. Yet they realize that a pure do-it-yourself approach will require a lot of time reinventing the wheel because they lack the *hows*. *Functionally*, the purely online InnovateU (independent learn-by-doing programs supported by online mentoring, similar to an online university) is the new solution they want.

Others know that they won't be able to sustain a program of transformation unless their feet are held to the fire with high-touch support, yet don't want to miss the opportunity of working with an expert resource. *Functionally*, Blended Programs, such as InnovateU+, composed of online programs plus webinars, and remote coaching or on-site support is the solution they want.

Emotionally, what every leader wants is an "easy button" that makes their business more successful so that they have more time for themselves and their family. I own that space in my clients' minds, because the straightforward and practical approaches I share deliver results in less time than they're spending on e-mail. Clients feel a sense of *relief* that they no longer have to reinvent the wheel and a sense of *anticipation* as a result of programs being delivered in bite-sized chunks at their convenience and time schedule. They gain a sense of *confidence* as they start to see themselves quickly and easily achieving the types of results I've outlined in this book. And they get a feeling of *exhilaration* as they see the transformation really taking shape and becoming sustainable. Each of these emotions are powerful differentiators for me versus other consultants.

All the Profit in Plain Sight Accelerators you'll access through the Rapid Results Resources referenced throughout the book are designed to offer business breakthroughs with high Functional Value and high Emotional Value, and are virtually impossible for other consultants to duplicate. My business model hits several of the Product Life Cycle Innovation opportunities, and rests squarely in the upper right of the Innovation Cocktail Framework.

Massive R&D was not required; just a willingness to reframe conventional approaches and offerings to better suit emerging client needs.

Your Takeaway: Rethink the Emotional Value you provide.

 Rapid Results Resources: Within the scope of this book, it's impossible for me to show you exactly how to develop "award winning cocktails" in the context of your unique company strengths. However, you can access numerous examples and the creative structure to refine your ideas and make them happen with the Innovation in Plain Sight Resources at www.ProfitInPlainSight. com/InnovateNow. You'll learn step-by-step details on how you can transform what you've learned in your Value Creation Conversations into low-risk, low-cost, high-value, hard-to-copy Innovation Cocktail Framework sweet spots and throughout the Product Life Cycle.

SOLUTION IN PLAIN SIGHT #3
Enter the Dragon to Foster Competitive Collaboration

There's a reason that the entrepreneurial *Dragon's Den* (*Shark Tank* in the US) is now a hit in over 14 countries — innovative, creative, entrepreneurial people are anxious for their ideas to be heard and to get the funding they need to change the world. They take a risk when their ideas are vetted, critiqued, or ridiculed. The PWC anecdote earlier illustrates that there's no reason not to create your own version in house.

Clear out your outdated "big idea" systems and policies, including suggestion boxes or formal idea-incentive programs. Replace them with an entrepreneurial culture using the Solutions in Plain Sight in this book to get employees actively engaging with customers and with other internal departments to find out what your customers are really trying to do and then help them do it more quickly and easily.

1. **Schedule Time for Innovation and Creativity:** The best companies in the world encourage staff to spend up to 20% of their time on Innovation and Creativity. A full day every week is out of reach for many employees and employers, which is why the strategies outlined here are designed to be completed in just 90 minutes once a week by cross-functional task forces composed of high-potential employees at every level. This process deliberately triggers applied creativity looking for high-impact solutions using rapid results brainstorming techniques and some very specifically structured creativity tools to evaluate and apply each Product Life Cycle element and each of the winning quadrants of the Innovation Cocktail Framework.

2. **Select Participants Shrewdly:** The key to success lies in crafting creative tension by understanding how to select the

right creative mix of participants, which is more than we can go into here, but building the right team is addressed in detail in every one of the Rapid Results Resources.

3. **Give Your Team Free Rein:** When you create a culture of constant creativity that systematically explores every low-risk, low-cost innovation opportunity, you and your team will transform your organization in three ways.

   - You'll achieve full-on engagement in opportunity spotting.

   - You'll quickly generate creative new ideas and prioritize those that are truly value-add.

   - You'll implement low-risk, low-cost innovations for impact and differentiate from your competition in powerful ways.

Get the Challenge of Creativity, Innovation, and Entrepreneurship out of a nice-to-do-someday approach by making it a regular part of your culture. Just get in the habit of using structured creativity tools to create opportunities to think differently in far less time than your team is currently spending on e-mail. You'll see results.

Innovation in Less Time than E-mail

An industrial manufacturer blended several innovation options into their in-house program.

Head office staff gathered weekly for Lunch-n-Learns while Gen X and Gen Y employees in remote offices used social media to brainstorm on an ongoing basis using the same Product Life Cycle and Innovation Cocktail structures. In just 90 minutes per week over a period of 90 days, both groups evaluated all 21 Low-Risk, Low-Cost Paths to Innovation and applied them to their business, based on the insights they'd gained in their Value Creation Conversations with customers. They short-listed seven ideas for further development and continued to collaborate to develop and implement their concepts.

While their process is still underway at the time of writing, the company was delighted to see how well the process promoted engagement, uncovered low-risk, low-cost opportunities they'd been overlooking, and identified future high-potential employees.

Your Takeaway: Make Innovation part of your everyday culture.

Use the Comprehensive Resources — Never Reinvent the Wheel

One of the biggest challenges leaders identify is that they simply don't have a framework for Innovation and Creativity. They want a process to ensure that they don't simply end up with a lot of weird and wonderful creative ideas that are impractical and fail to add any value, yet take up a lot of valuable time across the organization before fizzling out.

None of us were ever taught the right way to innovate. When asked to judge a recent innovation competition at a leading business school, I was appalled at the number of ideas that were "cool *inventions*" but did not fulfill any principles behind true value-add. It appeared that the curriculum had provided lots of examples of companies creating hit-it-out-of-the-ballpark products and services but, other than that, students were turned loose to simply use their imaginations to come up with so-called "innovations." That's the high-risk, high-cost road to failed products, rather than true Innovation, Creativity, and Entrepreneurship.

Transformation needs to be grounded in practical, proven frameworks that deliver results, if it's going to be sustainable. You don't have to reinvent any wheels. Simply use the systematic Profit in Plain Sight Framework and Resources to implement a straightforward approach to Innovation, Creativity, and Entrepreneurship that does not put the onus on your people to dream up new ideas, but rather allows them to step into their creativity in value-add ways.

Summary

You'll remain in the stagnation quadrant of "same products to the same customers" unless you master Innovation, Creativity, and Entrepreneurship and move to a place of growth by identifying value-add opportunities. You'll remain trapped in a world of increasing commoditization with relentless competition and increasing pressure on margins until you master the art of opportunity-spotting in your mature industry. Without frameworks and tools to drive the innovation process, you'll find yourself increasingly vulnerable to global competition that won't even be on your radar until it's too late and you'll spend too much time and money chasing blind alleys that don't deliver results.

Mastering Innovation, Creativity, and Entrepreneurship may seem like a "nice to do someday" when you and your team have more time. It isn't. You want to take action on this immediately, so that you can transform your marketplace safely, subtly, and in ways that are almost impossible for your competitors to copy. Every time you use an app on your smart phone, I want you to think about the person who saw an opportunity and ask yourself whether you'll be the one to provide your customers with the "apps" they need or whether you'll sink back into business as usual and allow one of your competitors to beat you to it.

As with all things in business, Innovation, Creativity, and Entrepreneurship is an ongoing process but it doesn't have to take a lot of time or cost a lot of money. It just needs to be embedded into your organizational culture as a part of the cycle of gaining insights from customers and turning them into value-add offerings with high Functional Value and high Emotional Value. You can spend a lot of time to figure out how to increase Innovation, Creativity, and Entrepreneurship on your own or you can use proven processes that deliver results.

You've seen how the 21 Low-Risk, Low-Cost Paths to Innovation can provide the structured exploration that's often missing from conventional innovation efforts, while actually unleashing the employee creativity in your organization that may be currently wasted or misdirected. The result is highly-applied value-add innovation that goes beyond "cool!" to commercialization.

You have a unique opportunity to combine deep customer insights (not superficial surveys or well-intentioned assumptions) with a focused process for surfacing the Functional and Emotional sweet spots when you create an environment structured for implementation rather than the inadvertent stifling of good ideas. You can uncover innovation that your customers will welcome and reward you for and that your competitors can't easily copy.

This Works. You Can Do It. You Will Succeed.

Take these Actions

Transformation takes more than awareness and good intentions.

Assessment	1. Take 11 minutes to complete the "Innovation in Plain Sight Assessment" at *www.ProfitInPlain Sight.com/Innovate* and pass the link along to your team so that you can compare notes.
Resource	2. Access your Innovation in Plain Sight Resources at *www.ProfitInPlainSight.com/InnovateNow*.
Action Item	3. Schedule a team meeting to: • Ask the Tough Love questions from the beginning of this Chapter. • Hold each other accountable when you hear tethered language or observe left-brain-dominated thinking regarding product development, innovation, or creativity. • Review your "Innovation in Plain Sight Assessment" results and compare notes. • Map your last three innovations to the Innovation Cocktail Framework and explore what that is telling you about your current approach to Innovation and Creativity.

Small Steps. Big Impact!

Five Minutes, Five Questions:
Reflect for Deeper Learning

Your first step is *internal* transformation, to identify what attitudes have already shifted and what behaviors will follow.

1. Which of my perceptions about the role of R&D need to shift as a result of seeing new paths to innovation?

   _____

2. What mechanisms and systems will we use to tap into the creativity and entrepreneurial spirit already within our organization and channel it towards value-add innovation?

   _____

   _____

3. How committed am I to fostering a culture of innovation by getting good people away from their everyday chores and giving them time to work on our Innovation and Creativity initiatives?

   _____

4. What needs to be put in place to deal with legacy "suggestion box" or similar systems, resistance to change, and "we've always done it this way" thinking?

   _____

   _____

5. What is my level of commitment to move from good intentions to implementation?

   _____

Inform. Inspire. Motivate. Transform.
Infuse. Enthuse.

Shift to Practicalities

Go beyond business as usual and begin your transformation by taking advantage of each one of these Rapid Results Resources at *www.ProfitInPlainSight.com/ProfitU.*

Checklist of Action Items

Assessment	1. Take 11 minutes to complete the "Profit in Plain Sight Assessment" at *www.ProfitInPlainSight.com/Profit* and pass the link along to your team so that you can compare notes.
	2. Take 11 minutes to complete the "Innovation in Plain Sight Assessment" at *www.ProfitInPlainSight.com/Innovate* and pass the link along to your team so that you can compare notes.
Resource	3. Access your "Who Has the Pricing Power" resources along with the "21 Safe, Sustainable Ways to Price for Value" at *www.ProfitInPlainSight.com/PriceforValue* to get a sense of where your best opportunities for acting on willingness-to-pay exist.
Resource	4. Commit to begin the process with the Value Creation Conversation Resources at *www.ProfitInPlainSight.com/GetInsights.*
Resource	5. Explore how you can make the right choices between CRS, CIS, CTS and CPS at *www.ProfitInPlainSight.com/Retain.*
Resource	6. Transform your Value Creation Conversations into Top-Line and Bottom-Line impact with the 5Rs for Proactively Managing Customer Profitability at *www.ProfitInPlainSight.com/GetProactive.*

Resource

7. Take immediate action in less time than you're currently spending on e-mail when you access the Rapid Results Resources to eliminate five factors that are causing 80 percent of your service costs at *www.ProfitInPlainSight.com/DeliverQuality*.

Resource

8. Access your Innovation in Plain Sight Resources at *www.ProfitInPlainSight.com/InnovateNow*.

Action Item

9. Schedule team meetings to:

   a. Ask the Tough Love questions from the beginning of each Chapter.

   b. Hold each other accountable when you hear "tethered" language or observe left-brain-dominated thinking about your customers.

   c. Decide how to divide and conquer the workload and complete your Value Creation Conversations.

   d. Review your "Profit in Plain Sight Assessment" results and compare notes on where your best opportunities for Passion, Profit, and Growth exist.

   e. Review your Pricing Power outcomes and the "21 Safe, Sustainable Ways to Price for Value."

   f. Start looking for your lettuce, everywhere in your business. Need help? *www.ProfitInPlain Sight.com/FindYourLettuce*.

   g. Start to have internal conversations regarding the implications of short-term dips in revenue and volume if firing a customer turns out to be the right strategy in some cases.

   h. Develop Sales-Service Plans to match your level of investment to the needs and potential of your customers.

i. Evaluate what would have to change in your organization in order to enable those on the front lines to say "yes" to any reasonable solution that would resolve issues on first contact. Is your organization brave enough to give it a try?

j. Bring your attention to the interactions you have as a customer in your business and personal life. Which experiences are bad, bland or good? What can you learn from them?

k. Commit to stop guessing what it will take to be the gold standard in your industry. Implement Value Creation Conversations and find out. Review the Apple Product Life Cycle example to identify questions and brainstorm its application to your organization.

l. Review your "Innovation in Plain Sight Assessment" results and compare notes.

m. Map your last three innovations to the Innovation Cocktail Framework and explore what that is telling you about your current approach to Innovation and Creativity.

10. Now that you see the systematic approach of Profit in Plain Sight coming together, you may be feeling a bit overwhelmed on how to get started, or not quite sure what's right for you. If you are committed to take action on your five stubborn market-driven challenges, I want to make it easy for you to take action. Send me an e-mail at *Mastery@ProfitInPlainSight.com*. I undertake a limited number of VIP intensive engagements to work hands-on with motivated leaders each year to help them implement the Profit in Plain Sight Framework. That level of personal support may be a better fit for you. Let's explore which of several blended learning options may best serve your needs.

You've seen how to use the Three Drivers of Transformation to establish base lines and trigger the Passion to transform your five stubborn market-driven challenges into Profit and Growth. You've explored the critical need to simply engage in uncommon, whole-brain-focused Value Creation Conversations to lock in Loyalty and Retention with the most valuable customers you've identified using your Customer Profitability Diamond. You've learned practical tactics and strategies to take action and drive tangible top- and bottom-line results using the 5Rs to Proactively Manage Customer Profitability with your team. You've discovered uncommon ways to develop your corporate Reputation for Quality and differentiate from your competition in meaningful ways. You've learned two simple frameworks that hold the key to Innovation and Creativity. And the success stories have shown you that it's all doable in less time than you're currently spending on e-mail. You've been exposed to uncommon right-brain thinking throughout the book and within the Rapid Results Resources.

This is the road map to accelerate profit and growth that you've been waiting for, supported by Rapid Result Resources to help you get the job done without ever having to reinvent the wheel.

This can't wait until "someday." You want to take action now with the systematic Profit in Plain Sight Framework and see tangible results that will show up on your next financials, and you want to take action before your next strategic planning session.

Impact Your Next Financial Reports With Passion, Profit, and Growth

Every insight you've developed will drive tangible Top-Line Growth and Bottom-Line Growth in Profits. Whether you will be reporting financials in 3 months, 6 months, 9 months or a year, you will see significant results when you take steps immediately to address your five stubborn market-driven challenges with the Rapid Results Resources.

Here's Your Road Map

THIS WEEK	Activate three Drivers of Transformation
	1. Benchmark your Return on People and set a new goal
	2. Calculate Your Profitable Customer Ratio
	3. Leverage the Power of Whole Brain Thinking

WITHIN 3 MONTHS

Get Insights in your first 90 days: Shine the spotlight on your Customer Profitability Diamond. Take just 90 minutes once a week and have your executive team conduct eyeball-to-eyeball Value Creation Conversations with your Retain and Ramp Up customers, generate deep insights, and understand their level of loyalty.

Restore your unprofitable customers to Breakeven or Better for immediate impact on your Bottom-Line Growth. Act on the new opportunities that will surface during your Value Creation Conversations to create rapid results for your Top-Line Growth.

WITHIN 6 MONTHS

Get Proactive in your second 90 days: Have a sales-and-marketing focused cross-functional team price for value using the willingness-to-pay that you've uncovered by asking the right questions in your Value Creation Conversations.

Take 90 minutes once a week to explore each one of the 21 Safe, Sustainable Ways to Price for Value, decide which ones will work best for your business, and implement. Implement your Reactivate Strategy, and develop your ongoing Sales-Service Plans to keep the momentum going. Your Top-Line Growth will swell and your bottom line will grow significantly.

WITHIN 9 MONTHS

Deliver quality in your third 90 days: Have a sales-and-operations focused cross-functional team oil your Tinman when you spend just 90 minutes once a week to get the sludge your customers have identified out of your system for good, or hold an intensive Root Cause Analysis Marathon for more rapid results.

When you use the Staple Yourself to an Experience Resources, you'll eliminate Unnecessary-Costs-to-Serve and boost your Bottom-Line a second time.

Let your customers know that you've taken action on their insights, and you'll likely see additional top-line impact as you build your Reputation for Quality and secure Customer Loyalty and Retention.

WITHIN 12 MONTHS

In your fourth 90 days: Simply use the 21 Paths to Low Cost, Low Risk Innovation to Find your Lettuce and trigger value-add Innovation and Creativity that will differentiate you from the competition, create competitive advantage that is almost impossible for your competitors to copy, and deliver additional Top-Line and Bottom-Line growth.

Congratulations! You've now increased your Top-Line Growth and earned the Bottom Line you need to fund your Business Bucket List for Growth so that you can reach your greater goals more quickly and easily. Along the way you've locked-in Customer Loyalty, built a corporate Reputation for Quality, and solved the Challenge of Innovation, Creativity, and Entrepreneurship.

And by devoting approximately 90 minutes just once a week, you've achieved all that in less time than you used to spend on e-mail!

Now its time to multiply your results and turn this into a way of doing business rather than simply a one-time event. To continue having all the resources you need to keep funding the blue sky investments for your Business Bucket List that you identified earlier, simply follow in the footsteps of successful business leaders and continue to follow this approach with as many customers as you have – your top 200, 500, 1000, or more.

You can take action on any of the practical recommendations and see impact on your business.

Drive Your Agenda for Future Strategic Planning

Strategic planning is all about leading your market by creating value for customers, building an organization that can deliver, and capturing that value in return so that you can grow and thrive. The insights from your Value Creation Conversations will profoundly shift your strategic thinking about the future of your business, how you differentiate from your customers, and how you create value that earns above-average profits. If you have a strategic planning session coming up within the next 12 months, investing well in advance to generate Whole-Brain Thinking using the resources outlined in this book is essential.

It's Where All the Fun Is

Most importantly, this is not more work. Work happens in the chair behind your desk. All the fun in your business is on the *other* side of your desk — connecting with customers to creatively solve their problems and be rewarded for doing so! Don't miss out any longer. Get out from behind your desk. Go and have insightful conversations with customers that get your creative juices flowing again. Set new goals and see the level of energy go up across your organization as you start to achieve what you never thought you could, almost effortlessly.

Shine the spotlight, stop the bleeding, oil your Tinman, find your lettuce, concoct some cocktails, and just get back to doing what you love to do — solving problems for customers better than your competition can and making a bundle of well-earned profit with integrity doing it.

This Works. You Can Do It. You Will Succeed.

Passion. Profit. Growth. What are you waiting for?

Right now, only one action is required. Go to *www.ProfitIn PlainSight.com/ProfitU and make a commitment to get started.*

How Will You Transform Your Passive Book Learning into Impact?

Awareness and Good Intentions Don't Turn Up on Your Income Statement

No business has a remote control.
You have to move to change the channel.

How much time and energy would you recapture if you slowly but surely took steps to address each of the five stubborn market-driven challenges as outlined in this book?

What kind of impact could you have on your business and your marketplace by implementing each of the Solutions in Plain Sight instead of closing this book and returning to status quo?

What Possibilities will open up when you make the commitment and help everyone else in your organization focus as much time on driving your business forward as you're wasting on e-mail today?

Right now you have just one decision to make. Are you going to put this book on your shelf with all the others or take the next 90 minutes to begin your transformation to Passion, Profit, and Growth?

I said earlier that you can lead a horse to water, but you can't make it drink. What you can do is to make the horse thirsty or to make the water sweeter. I hope I've done both — whetted your appetite to finally get traction on the Challenges that have been holding your company back and given you the sweetener by making it simple, straightforward, and actionable — in less time than your organization is spending on e-mail.

It's time to shift from learning to action.

Take Just Three Steps

1. **Go to** *www.ProfitInPlainSight.com/ProfitU* **to access value-add Resources and the Profit in Plain Sight Framework**. Simply follow the step-by-step instructions to start implementing each Profit and Growth Accelerator and transform your five stubborn market-driven challenges into Passion, Profit, and Growth.

2. **Or, connect with me one-on-one to build a customized road map for results.** Now that you see the systematic approach of the Profit in Plain Sight Framework coming together, you may be feeling a bit overwhelmed on how to get started, or not quite sure what's right for you. If you are committed to take action on your five stubborn market-driven challenges, I want to make it easy for you to take action. Send me an e-mail at *Mastery@ProfitInPlainSight.com*. I undertake a limited number of VIP Intensive engagements to work hands-on with motivated leaders each year to help them implement the systematic Profit in Plain Sight Framework. That level of personal support may be a better fit for you. Let's explore which of several options may best serve your needs.

3. **Demonstrate leadership with others who need *Profit in Plain Sight* at** *www.ProfitInPlainSight.com/Share*.

   - **Gift a copy of this book to everyone in your organization and get them on the same page**. You can spend a lot of time explaining or make a small investment in inspiring your employees to achieve more by having them read this book and/or attend in a keynote at your next leadership retreat or annual sales meeting. You are thirsty for more, aren't you?

- **Gift a copy to each of your customers.** They really don't need another baseball cap or golf shirt with your logo. They don't need another lunch, golf game, or event ticket. What they really need is to learn the secrets of building a strong and sustainable company so they can keep doing business with you. They need a copy of this book with your *Compliments of* imprint on the front cover. You do want them to succeed, don't you?

- **Gift a copy to your suppliers**. Wouldn't it be great if they started delivering a better experience by listening for deep insights into how they could better serve you? Imagine how much time *you'd* save if *they* were getting it right the first time. You do want them to make your life easier, don't you?

- **Help your community or industry association make this information available to their members**. Gift a copy of the book to the Executive Director or CEO of industry or business associations you belong to, or suggest that they book a keynote speech for their next conference. You do want to demonstrate leadership in your community of peers, correct?

Go to *www.ProfitInPlainSight.com/Share* for economical bulk purchase options or to book a great keynote at *www.Anne CGraham.com*.

Let's Build a Community of Practice that Makes a Difference

With your help, we can build a community of practice that puts our economy back on a value-based, strong, sustainable footing now and builds for our future. Let's all take a small action that makes a profound difference.

"Employ your time in improving yourself by other men's writings so that you shall come easily by what others have labored hard for."

~Socrates~

Put the Big Rocks in First

How to Transform Your Business in Less Time than You're Spending on E-mail

Time is not our problem. Fear and lack of focus is the only thing holding us back.

Folks, I already shared the story of the big rocks in the Overview of Part II, Shift to Practicalities. Let me just provide a final bit of tough love and reinforce that the "big rocks" are anything and everything to do with *the one and only source of cash flow* in your business — your customers — and *those who make it happen* — your people. All else is trivial. Those big rocks need to become your first priority every day. Period.

A day that starts with e-mail has little time for big rocks.

busy work

e-mail

A day that starts with big rocks transforms your business more quickly and easily than you can imagine.

Small shift. Big impact.

Most of us start our day with e-mail, and unless you're in the order entry department, e-mail does *not* create Passion, Profit, and Growth in your business. Instead, it has you spending valuable time working *everyone else's agenda*. Especially if you're in a leadership role, it's your responsibility to proactively *set* the agenda, not simply respond.

Here's a little exercise to get you thinking:

- Write down the time that you usually start your workday:
  _____

- Write down the time that is 90 minutes later than that:
  _____

- Ask yourself if your world would end or your business
  implode if you did not check e-mail until the later time.

Executives polled say they spend a minimum of 90-120 minutes on e-mail *every day*. It's easy to start your day that way, coffee in hand. But it's not how you transform your business into a powerhouse of Passion, Profit, and Growth.

Instead, spend those first 90 minutes having a Value Creation Conversation with a customer, working with a team to identify Root Cause issues to get the sludge out of your system, brainstorming Price-for-Value options, pursuing an Innovation agenda, or Proactively Managing Customer Profitability on an ongoing basis.

For starters, don't even do it every day — do this *just once a week* in the beginning.

You don't have to choose between e-mail and your customers; simply put the big rocks in first, and e-mail and other tasks will fill the other spaces, just as the pebbles and sand do in the illustration above.

Here's another little exercise to shift your mind-set and transform your business.

If you work a traditional 8:30 a.m to 5:00 p.m. day (Are you laughing at the thought?), you have at least two 90-minute windows in every morning and two in every afternoon.

With four windows every day, five days a week, you end up with *260 valuable windows* in every 13-week quarter. No leader, manager, or individual contributor I've worked with has *ever* been able

	4 Monday	5 Tuesday	6 Wednesday	7 Thursday	8 Friday
8am					
	Big Rocks	Big Rocks	Big Rocks	Big Rocks	Big Rocks
9⁰⁰					
10⁰⁰					
	Big Rocks	Big Rocks	Big Rocks	Big Rocks	Big Rocks
11⁰⁰					
12pm					
1⁰⁰	Big Rocks	Big Rocks	Big Rocks	Big Rocks	Big Rocks
2⁰⁰					
3⁰⁰	Big Rocks	Big Rocks	Big Rocks	Big Rocks	Big Rocks
4⁰⁰					
5⁰⁰					

to fill each of those 260 windows with high-value activities. You'll find a lot of "white space" when you do this exercise — even if you just schedule one Big Rocks window in each day, you're still way ahead of the game.

So your problem is not *time*, it's *focus*. Too many of us work long hours because we fritter our day away with "stuff" rather than doing what matters (I've been there too).

Guess what. Even with the Big Rocks approach, there's lots of time for "stuff" in your day. See the white space? That's where your pebbles and sand (and e-mail) fit.

With 260 windows available in every quarter, I'm only asking you to devote about 13 of those to transforming your business. You're probably spending at least 65 of those valuable windows just on e-mail. Does that make sense to you? Will you shift your priorities and transform your business? Only you can decide.

Rapid Results Resources: Take this out for a test drive. Access the "Put the Big Rocks in First Toolkit" to map out your next quarter at www. ProfitInPlainSight.com/Focus. I dare you to see if you can fill 260 windows with high quality activities.

Transform Your Business in Less Time than You're Spending on E-mail

You don't need to reinvent any wheels. You don't need to create yet another monster project that your busy team will resent and resist. All you want to do is implement this proven systematic framework, in small, bite-size chunks on a regular basis. Every Resource will show you exactly how to make this work for you.

This Works. You Can Do It. You Will Succeed

Take these Actions

Transformation takes more than awareness and good intentions.

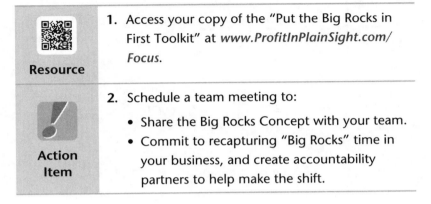

Resource	1. Access your copy of the "Put the Big Rocks in First Toolkit" at *www.ProfitInPlainSight.com/Focus*.
Action Item	2. Schedule a team meeting to: • Share the Big Rocks Concept with your team. • Commit to recapturing "Big Rocks" time in your business, and create accountability partners to help make the shift.

Small Steps. Big Impact!

 Reflect for Deeper Learning

1. How am I feeling about the way I currently spend my days?

_____

_____

2. What Possibilities do I see to transform our business in less time than I'm spending on e-mail?

_____

_____

3. How committed am I to making it happen?

_____

_____

A Solution in Plain Sight

Here's the answer to the brain teaser from the beginning of the book that asked you to find the form of transportation.

I've simply reframed the images you saw.

What form of transportation do you see now?

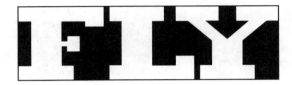

Of course, it's FLY.

We're all used to seeing black writing on a white page and this example reversed that. Without seeing things a little differently, most people can't spot anything but the black shapes. But once we're shown the Solution in Plain Sight, we find it hard to go back to old ways of seeing things. Try it now. Go back and look at the original image again. Can you see anything BUT the word FLY, clearly spelled out?

That's what *Profit in Plain Sight* will do for your business, so don't put this book down and go back to business as usual! Once you've reframed what you're used to seeing, what appears "in plain sight" will be impossible to ignore.

So pick up from page 6 and keep reading — it's time for your business to fly!

Acknowledgments

With sincere thanks and appreciation for:

- the managers and leaders throughout my career from whom I learned so much ...
- my employees who inspired me with their passion to be the best ...
- the many colleagues who have supported my goals ...
- my MBA and PhD students at the University of British Columbia who helped me learn just as much from their questions as they ever did from my answers ...
- the many authors whose works made a difference to my thinking ...
- my valued clients who helped me improve my business as I helped them improve theirs ...
- the hundreds of members of TEC/Vistage Canada for endlessly title-testing with me and subsequently sharing their stories and experiences as they implemented these strategies ...
- my incredibly talented marketing interns, Rachel Raffa, Maude Olivia Pires, and Sheen Sagalongos ...
- my friends who are there in good times and bad ...
- and, of course, my family, who have been with me throughout the journey.

With thanks and gratitude to those who reviewed the initial manuscript and made it better:

Hugh Alley	Chris Dennis	Catherine Osler
Laura Aveledo	Heather MacKenzie	Jason Ray
Pat Bjerrisgaard	Leslie Meingast	Renee Safrata
Jim Bogusz	Jens Nilausen	Jim Sellner
Al Dhalla	George Noroian	Doug Wagner

To my editor, Catherine Leek, whose expertise was invaluable, thank you.

To Kim Monteforte, whose design efforts added the essential spice, thank you.

Recommended Resources

Burck, Charles and Larry Bossidy, Ram Charan. *Execution: The Discipline of Getting Things Done* (New York: Crown Publishing Group, 2002)

Charan, Ram. *Global Tilt: Leading Your Business Through the Great Economic Power Shift* (New York: Crown Publishing Group, 2013)

Christensen, Clayton M. *The Innovator's Dilemma: When New Technologies Cause Great Firms to Fail* (Boston: Harvard Business Review Press, 1997)

Colvin, Geoff. *Talent Is Overrated: What Really Separates World-class Performers from Everybody Else* (New York: Portfolio, 2008)

Colvin, Geoff. *The Upside of the Downturn* (New York: Portfolio, 2009)

Godin, Seth. *The Icarus Deception: How High Will You Fly?* (New York: Portfolio, 2012)

Hamel, Gary. *Leading the Revolution: How to Thrive in Turbulent Times by Making Innovation a Way of Life* (Boston: Harvard Business Review Press, 2003)

Hamel, Gary. *What Matters Now* (Hoboken: Wiley, 2012)

Harnish, Verne. *Mastering the Rockefeller Habits* (New York: Select, 2002)

Heath, Chip and Dan Heath. *Decisive: How to Make Better Choices in Life and Work.* (Toronto: Random House of Canada, 2013)

Heath, Chip and Dan Heath. *Made to Stick: Why Some Ideas Survive and Others Die* (New York: Random House Publishing Group, 2007)

Heath, Chip and Dan Heath. *Switch: How to Change Things When Change Is Hard* (Toronto: Random House of Canada, 2010)

Kotter, John P. *Leading Change* (Boston: Harvard Business Review Press, 2012)

Kotter, John P. *On What Leaders Really Do* (Boston: Harvard Business Review Press, 2012)

Lafley, A.G. and Roger L. Martin. *Playing to Win: How Strategy Really Works* (Boston: Harvard Business Review Press, 2013)

Lencioni, Patrick M. *The Advantage: Why Organizational Health Trumps Everything Else in Business* (Hoboken: Wiley, 2012)

Lencioni, Patrick M. *The Five Dysfunctions of a Team: A Leadership Fable* (Hoboken: Wiley, 2002)

MacKay, Harvey. *Swim with the Sharks without Being Eaten Alive: Outsell, Outmanage, Outmotivate, and Outnegotiate Your Competition* (New York: HarperCollins Publishers, 2005)

Martin, Roger L. *The Opposable Mind: How Successful Leaders Win through Integrative Thinking* (Boston: Harvard Business Review, 2007)

Mauborgne, Renee, and W. Chan Kim. *Blue Ocean Strategy: How to Create Uncontested Market Space and Make the Competition Irrelevant* (Boston: Harvard Business Review Press, 2005)

Peters, Thomas. *The Little Big Things: 163 Ways to Pursue Excellence* (New York: HarperCollins Publishers, 2012)

Pink, Daniel H. *Drive: The Surprising Truth about What Motivates Us* (New York: Riverhead, 2011)

Seybold, Patricia B. *Outside Innovation: How Your Customers Will Co-Design Your Company's Future* (New York: HarperCollins Publishers, 2006)

Slywotzky, Adrian. *The Art of Profitability* (New York: Grand Central Publishing, 2003)

Stengel, Jim. *Grow: How Ideals Power Growth and Profit at the World's Greatest Companies* (New York: Crown Publishing Group, 2011)

Zook, Chris and James Allen. *Profit from the Core: A Return to Growth in Turbulent Times* (Boston: Harvard Business Review Press, 2010)

Zook, Chris and James Allen. *Repeatability: Build Enduring Businesses for a World of Constant Change* (Boston: Harvard Business Review Press, 2012)

Industry Week magazine is a valuable resource for success stories of leadership and excellence in the manufacturing sector. Find it online at: www.industryweek.com

Solutions in Plain Sight Radio shares the simple AHA! Moments learned by business experts in the school of hard knocks that can really move the needle in your business: *www.SolutionsInPlain Sight.com*

Index

C

turbulent, 21, 51

turnarounds, 138

Twitter, 95

U

underestimate, 25, 127

underserved, 256, 259

university, 40
    of British Columbia, 96, 247
    online, 267

Unnecessary-Costs-to-Serve, 9, 72-73,
    113, 118, 145, 151, 213, 215, 223,
    226, 228, 282

unprofitable, 61, 63, 65-66, 68-69,
    71-76, 78-79, 117-118, 187-192,
    194-203, 206-209, 211, 264, 281

untether, 84-86, 88, 90-91, 101-102,
    106, 110, 114, 125, 159, 189, 216,
    221, 242

V

Value-add, 7-8, 10-11, 21, 32, 41, 43,
    44, 45, 47, 56, 65, 72, 74, 78, 87,
    89, 96, 104, 122, 124, 126-127,
    129, 131-132, 134-135, 139, 151,
    158, 161, 166-167, 169-173, 175,
    177-178, 180-181, 188, 196, 202-
    204, 214, 227-228, 230, 240-243,
    248-253, 257, 260, 267, 270-273,
    275, 282, 286

value chain, 253, 259

Value Creation Conversations, 40,
    116-119, 124, 131, 136, 138-151,
    153-154, 155, 161-162, 167,
    168-173, 175-179, 182, 199, 204,
    207, 222, 224, 226, 228-229, 231,
    235, 236, 244-245, 248, 253, 257,
    263-263, 266, 268, 271, 277-281,
    283, 290

Value driver, 152

Value Gap, 174-175, 245

Vampire Customers, 73, 75, 185, 187,
    189, 191-197, 200, 205-208, 211

vendor, 130-131, 138, 146, 218,
    262-263

VIP, 279, 286

vision, 29

Visual/Spatial Learning, 98-99

Voice of the Customer, 45, 142,
    144, 151

volume, 55, 58, 60, 87, 99, 125, 151,
    178, 185, 187, 189, 192, 194, 206,
    209, 232, 260, 278

vulnerable, 125, 207, 265, 272

W

Walkman, 246-247

Watson, Thomas J., 2

Welch, Jack, 216

Wet Diaper, 7, 10-11, 14, 86

What's on Hold Checklist, 38, 39

Who Has the Pricing Power, 179,
    182, 277-278

Who's Who, 67-69, 74, 79, 82, 109,
    177, 194, 200, 204

Whole-Brain Thinking, 7, 9, 19-20,
    22-23, 83, 88, 91-101, 103-105,
    107, 109, 137, 260, 283

Willingness-to-Pay, 72, 118, 159,
    168, 169, 176-178, 181-182, 184

Wizard of Oz, 168, 214, 226, 232

worksheet, 43-44, 47

workshop, 118

Y

YouTube, 95

Z

Zipcar, 265

Quick Order Form

For faster service, order at *www.ProfitInPlainSight.com/Share*

☎ **Toll Free (855)-259-9858**

@ **Email Orders: orders@ProfitInPlainSight.com**

✉ **LVI Publishing, 4132–349 West Georgia St., Vancouver, BC V6B 3Z6**

Please send the following books:

QTY	ITEM	PRICE
	Profit In Plain Sight	29.99
	Total*	

Payment options:

☐ **VISA**   ☐ MasterCard   ☐ AMERICAN EXPRESS

Name	
Card Number	
CVC Code	Expiry Date
Card Holder Name (please print)	
Signature	

Please send more FREE information on:

☐ eBooks   ☐ Learn-by-Doing Programs   ☐ Keynote Speaking   ☐ Consulting

Name	
Address	
City	
State/Province	Zip/Postal Code
Telephone	
Email Address	

*Sales tax and/or shipping charges may apply.

Note: Bulk orders may be eligible for special discounts and your own personalized imprint. E-mail *Bulk@ProfitInPlainSight.com* for details.